London Patidars

International Library of Sociology

Founded by Karl Mannheim

Editor: John Rex, University of Aston in Birmingham

Arbor Scientiae
Arbor Vitae

A catalogue of the books available in the **International Library of Sociology** and other series of Social Science books published by Routledge & Kegan Paul will be found at the end of this volume.

London Patidars

A case study in urban ethnicity

Harald Tambs-Lyche
University of Bergen

Routledge & Kegan Paul
London, Boston and Henley

First published in 1980
by Routledge & Kegan Paul Ltd
39 Store Street, London WC1E 7DD,
Broadway House, Newtown Road,
Henley-on-Thames, Oxon RG9 1EN and
9 Park Street, Boston, Mass. 02108, USA
Printed in Great Britain by
Redwood Burn Ltd, Trowbridge and Esher

British Library Cataloguing in Publication Data

Tambs-Lyche, Harald

London Patidars.
1. Patidars in London
I. Title
301.45'19'1470421   DA125.P/   80–40636

ISBN 0 7100 8471 4

272, 235

B/19192

To my Father
whose dedication to social affairs inspired this work

... when he suddenly saw Piglet sitting in his best arm chair, he could only stand there rubbing his head and wondering whose house he was in.

'Hallo, Piglet', he said, 'I thought you were out.'

'No', said Piglet, 'it's you who were out, Pooh.'

'So it was', said Pooh, 'I knew one of us was.'

A.A. Milne, 'The House at Pooh Corner', Methuen, 1928, p. 2

Contents

Contents

Foreword

When I returned to the Midlands and specifically to
Coventry in 1970, I was interested to learn that a number
of social anthropologists were at work studying the local
Asian communities. More particularly, I was delighted to
learn that a graduate student of Fredrik Barth of Bergen
was studying Gujarati merchants. Knowing the way in
which Barth's thinking in the theory of social anthropology had opened up a new dimension in the subject, I
expected the work of his students to be interesting. The
essay which follows on London Patidars in no way dis-
appoints me. Brief though it is, I believe that it opens
up new perspectives on the study of ethnic minorities in
Britain and in other advanced industrial countries.

British and European literature on immigration,
minorities and race relations is extraordinarily
unsophisticated and theoretically and methodologically
backward. The first response of sociologists and
interested laymen to the arrival of large numbers of West
Indian, Indian and Pakistani immigrants in Britain in the
1950s and 1960s was, in fact, a crude sort of Owenite
environmentalism. Problems of the immigrant communities
were reduced to the kinds of problems which could be
assessed by public health inspectors and dealt with by
simple parliamentary legislation or municipal action.
At a slightly higher level, a statistically empiricist
approach was adopted showing the differential access to
life-chances of immigrants and native groups. A third
approach, 'Colour and Citizenship', concerned itself with
the impact of immigration on British economic and
political life and particularly on the values of the
British political system.

Finally, and in contrast to the approach of 'Colour
and Citizenship', there was a reversion to the study of
discrimination, looked at much more from the point of view

ix

of the deprivation and suffering which it imposes upon
the immigrant community.

Harald Tambs-Lyche's approach switches attention from
the problems of British society and the subordination of
empirical research to the questions of social justice to
asking the all-important questions: Who are the
immigrants? What are their goals and ideals? What are
the constraints under which they make choices? What
choices do they make? This is in the tradition of the
work of Fredrik Barth, and before that directly in the
tradition of Max Weber's use of the action frame of
reference. It is surprising how little this tradition
has affected the sociology of ethnic group relations,
since one would have thought that a first question to be
asked before questions about discrimination become
meaningful was that of what various immigrant groups
actually thought about their circumstances.

Tambs-Lyche's Patidars are described in these pages as
having certain primary, secondary and tertiary statuses
both within their own society, the relatively closed
society of the Patidar community, and within the
encompassing society, which, given their goals and the
power at their disposal, has to be treated as brute
environment. This, however, by no means precludes the
possibility that immigrants may exploit social niches
available to them and, in terms of their own values, do
very well. The Patidars of Charottar who participated
in the great Indian diaspora set in train by British
colonialism went to all corners of the earth, particularly
to Fiji and East Africa. Most of the London Patidars
came to England via East Africa. The experience which
they gained during their migration enhanced the change
which they were undergoing from being land-owners and
warriors to being merchants.

In their contemporary culture, to seize business
opportunities wherever they are to be found and to pursue
business success has become an ideal rather akin to the
Protestant ethic as described by Weber, but considerably
complicated by the fact that money gained through work or
commercial enterprise may be converted into other kinds
of generalized means within the secondary statuses which
the individual may have as landlord, broker and so on.
An extraordinarily interesting and complex picture of
the interaction between Patidar values and the social
situation of immigrants arises from the case studies
presented here.

Like most Scandinavian sociologists who have dealt
with minority problems, Tambs-Lyche is extraordinarily
sensitive to the way in which questions of value affect

social research from the stage of elementary perception
to the stage of theory. He is very clear in confessing
that the Patidar ideals which he encountered were too
unpleasantly reminiscent of the European petit-bourgeois
to gain his sympathy. None the less, like a good
anthropologist, he enters into relations with those whom
he studies and learns about social structure from the
inside.

By so doing he probably makes a better contribution in
the long run to the understanding of questions of
discrimination and social justice than those who begin
simply with the study of austere statistical indices.
We need many more studies like this in Britain and in
Europe. One hopes that this one may trigger off a whole
series and that sociologists might learn something of the
kinds of interaction which are going on before their eyes
and are obscured by the more official reaction to social
reality.

John Rex

Acknowledgments

I should like to thank all those who have contributed to
this book by their willingness to supply data, to discuss
theoretical points, and in other ways. The work was
carried out in many different places, and the list below
is far from complete. My thanks, therefore, to those not
mentioned, as well as to the following:

To my host, friend and main informant, Shantu Ram
Patel and his family.

To my other landlord in London, Ramesh B. Patel and
his household.

To Praful Patel, Mr Solanki of 'Garavi Gujarat', B.C.
Raj, Bhagwan Soaham, G.G. Patel and his two sons in
Coventry, to the keeper of the Swaminarayana Temple in
Islington, to Mukund R. Patel, and to all the Patidars
in London, Coventry and Rugby to whom I was an inquisi-
tive, and, no doubt, sometimes embarrassing visitor.

To my friends Jagdish, Ashwin, Jay, Sanjay and Sarwan,
as well as Anil and Ashok, Bhogilal and Kirit.

To Professor A.C. Mayer who took me under his wing at
the School of Oriental and African Studies, and to the
participants in his group studying immigrants from the
Indian subcontinent, especially Badr-ud-din Dahya and
Audrey Boorne, who also helped me in many other ways.

To other anthropologists at SOAS, especially to Dr
Abner Cohen, Dr Barbara Ward and Dr Stephan Feuchtwang.
As Dr Cohen was absent during a large part of my stay,
I should emphasize that his influence was no less
important for that; I owe him a great intellectual debt,
even though this influence was mediated to a considerable
extent through the minds of others.

To my student friends at SOAS, first of all to Bengt-
Erik Borgstrøm, whose criticism influenced my work a
great deal; and to Rohit Barot, Roger Hallam, and Mark
Thompson, whose work on similar problems proved a constant

inspiration. To Mark, also thanks for much help during
my Coventry stay.

To Suneet Chopra, Bharpoor Brar Singh and Mike York,
also at SOAS, and to Mike Lyons at the University of
Aberdeen.

To Professor John Rex at Warwick University, who gave
me the opportunity to take part in a series of seminars
arranged there at the time, and whose criticism proved
very fruitful.

To friends in London, especially to Richard and Ruth.

To Anne.

To the anthropologists at Oslo University, whose
criticism helped me considerably.

To my teachers at the Department of Anthropology here
in Bergen, especially to Jan-Petter Blom who introduced
me to the subject, to Fredrik Barth, who followed the
progress of the fieldwork closely and gave me every kind
of advice and assistance, and to Gunnar Haaland, who, as
a tutor, has been largely instrumental in making some
kind of a thesis out of my ideas.

To everyone else at the Department.

To Merete Blinkenberg Nielsen for typing the manuscript
and correcting many of my mistakes in the process.

To my parents, whose help has been of a critical as
well as a personal kind.

Last, I hope that the conclusions reached may prove
of some value to the Patidars themselves in their
attempts to achieve a better adaptation to their new
society.

Introduction

Before any systematic treatment of the main theme of this
book is attempted, I want to give the reader some idea of
how the community studied presented itself to me as an
outsider and as a newcomer. There is a strong tradition
in anthropology concerning the necessity of the 'cultural
shock' as an initiation into the society studied (see e.g.
Bohannan, 1963, pp.7-14; Berreman, 1962, p.5; Freilich
(ed.), 1970, passim). Even if the present fieldwork was
perhaps not undertaken in a very exotic setting, I
certainly did experience something of the kind. England
itself was quite new to me, as I had visited the country
only once before. But my 'cultural shock' was not due to
the setting. Rather, it was due to the values communi-
cated by my Indian friends; the 'atmosphere' of the
community as I perceived it; and the way in which personal
relationships developed in unexpected ways. All this,
given my different background, seemed strange, unfamiliar
and, at first, unpleasant.

It might be held that all this personal experience is
quite irrelevant to the factual results of the fieldwork,
which, taken in themselves, are what really matter. But
I would disagree, for such a view is, I think, too
simplistic. My argument in this book is based not only
upon 'bare facts' but also to a large extent on my
interpretation of them as a fieldworker. In particular,
the 'merchant ideology' of which I am talking clearly
cannot be observed directly. The concept was, in the
beginning, no more than an impression, and though I set
about testing it, this impression clearly directed much
of my work from then on.

This was my approach. I can think of at least two
alternatives, both of them more inductive in character
and so, perhaps, less likely to be influenced by the
fieldworker's prejudices. One alternative would be to

1

assemble vast amounts of data on strategies followed by individuals, as well as the circumstances in which they were followed. Taking for granted that there is a rational relation between the strategies followed and the values sought, one might, to a certain extent, deduce the values. But in order to rise above complete triviality, the number of cases would have to be quite high.

The other alternative would be very intensive study of face-to-face interaction, thus assembling a large mass of data on how people communicate their values. Again, from this kind of study, values might perhaps be deduced by applying a method similar to Goffman's for interpretation of the data. This method, too, would need a considerable volume of data to be anything like conclusive in itself.

In the event, I did not find such intensive study very convenient. I was accepted into the community as a student of Gujarati language and customs, and I was accepted, too, as a dependant of my landlord. I felt that I was accepted as a friend and as at least a make-believe member of the community. I do not think that I could have taped the conversations at which I was present without spoiling the atmosphere. Neither would it have been easy to take notes at the time. I therefore had to rely chiefly on post hoc notes, and to remember afterwards what had been said and done. Often this involved trying to describe a whole evening of eager discussions. Nobody could claim, in this situation, not to be influenced in his notes by his general conceptions of his informants' values and the ideology into which he expected it all to fit.

It may well be asked what I mean by ideology? Later, I shall discuss the model I am using. Here, a short statement will perhaps suffice. I shall take ideology to mean the scales for evaluation of alternative courses of action open to an actor. Through interaction within a certain culture some agreement as to evaluations and thus to ideology becomes necessary, and so it is reasonable to say that these scales for evaluation are to some extent similar for actors within a certain culture. Thus individual actors may, I would hold, disagree with certain evaluations, but can hardly disregard them. Looking at ideology in this way, it becomes meaningful to try to identify a common stock of evaluations as between actors, and it is such a stock of evaluations that I shall call, in the case of the London Patidars, a 'merchant ideology'.

My idea of this 'merchant ideology' was very much based on initial impressions. These impressions, then,

are important, whether or not they are correct. Not only
does my understanding of the ideology depend upon them;
all the data that again depend upon understanding the
ideology, all this mass of 'soft' data, stems from them.
And not only are these data influenced by my own
prejudices and preconceptions; it is these very prejudices
and preconceptions which, confronted with and corrected
by further experience, themselves form the basis of my
understanding of the society.

My 'cultural shock', then, is relevant to my presentation of data. What did it feel like to enter the
community?

The prejudices inherent in this position all played
their part in my interpretation of the ideology I found
among the London Patidars. To be honest, I did not like
their views. What was it that I reacted so strongly
against? It was, probably, above all, an ideology which
I immediately codified as 'petit-bourgeois'. In doing
this I was using concepts from my own culture that were,
to me, very heavily value-laden. In fact this word had
always stood as an idiom for whatever seemed to me
unsympathetic and perhaps worthy of contempt. In trying
to sort out the hows and whys of this ideology, I therefore found myself fighting my own prejudice, trying to
see the ideology of my friends and informants as a result
of and as a tool of social process rather than as an
ideology opposed to my own within my own culture. (1)

The reason I tried so hard was, more than anything,
the sheer friendliness and helpfulness of my main
'informant', whom I shall call Anilbhai. I could not
have written this book without his constant assistance,
not only as an 'informant' but as a friend and 'pseudo-
father' in the situation. Throughout my stay I felt
that his house had indeed become my London home. For
most of my twelve-month visit he was my landlord, and I
learned more from him and his family than from everybody
else put together. So the warm welcome I was given made
me try to break through my prejudice to a better understanding of the ideology of the Patidars I met in London.

Helped by Badr-ud-din Dahya and other friends, I was
trying to find a room with someone of the community
(which, at that time, I thought of as the Gujarati
community), when one day, walking along the main street
of an inner London suburb, I scanned one of the numerous
advertisement boards outside a shop. The advertisement
read something like this:
   Rooms to let with Indian meals
   Enquire to Mr Anilbhai Patel
   (And the address).

Not only did the Indian food sound promising, but Patel,
I knew, was a name almost certainly to be that of a
Gujarati.

Going to the house that day, however, I was told that
all the rooms were already let, the advertisement, in
fact, being an old one. The shopkeeper must have
forgotten to take it down.

I explained my problems more fully: I was learning
Gujarati and wanted to live in a Gujarati house. 'Well,'
said the young boy who had answered the door, 'I should
talk to Mr Patel himself if I were you. He has a lot of
contacts, and maybe he knows about some other place.'

So I went downstairs to where Mr Patel lived. (He had
retained for his own use the basement and the ground-
floor front room. All the other rooms were by now let.)
Mr Patel was one big smile: 'Thirteen years I have been
in this country. Nobody ever tried to learn my language.'
I was given tea and biscuits and had to tell him everything about my background. He, for his part, told me
quite a bit about himself. His father had gone to Fiji
after the First World War, and had been doing quite well
as a businessman. At home, at that period, times were
bad; his father had died young, and the family lands had
to be mortgaged. Mr Patel himself was born in Fiji.
Before the Second World War, his father had returned to
India, to Nadiad in the district of Kaira, in the land
called Charottar in central Gujarat. He bought back the
family lands. Mr Patel, however, had found no future in
India: 'No money to be made from the land these days.'
In 1955 he had come to England, to Huddersfield, taking
up work as a car painter. He later moved to London and
brought his wife and children over. In 1966 he bought
the house in which we were then sitting: 'Close to
schools - good for the boys' education.'

All this and more he told me, and then made me an
offer: 'If you want to, you can stay in the boys' room.
A relative of the wife, she was living there last year.
I'll let you stay there, and you can pay me £4 a week -
food and all included. You'll be just like part of the
family.'

I accepted. I was to stay there in the boys' room
until maybe one of the lodgers moved. This in fact
happened later that autumn.

Aku and Baku, as the boys were called, became very
good friends of mine. They also became excellent
informants, telling me about school, about friends, about
their view of almost everything, they became my teachers
to a very large extent. In their English homework I
tried to reciprocate by giving them what assistance I

could, but there was little I could do: they both improved
their written English tremendously, fully through their
own efforts, until it was better than mine. We went to
museums and other places together, and had quite a good
time. On one of these occasions one - to my mind,
surprising - incident happened: I tried to buy us some
soft drinks or sweets, but found them completely unwilling
to accept anything. It was not pride; what was argued was
the stupidity of spending money on such useless things.
'We can have some tea and biscuits at home, it's better
and cheaper,' Aku said. But home was still hours away.

This was not the only time I was surprised by the
boys' frugality. Once, I had bought myself a car magazine
(cars being an old interest of mine). 'But what do you
want it for?' 'Four shillings - My God!' were two of
Aku's comments. I was sufficiently influenced by these
comments not to buy any more magazines. I felt I had
better abstain from such luxurious spending in their
presence; and I really felt a bit silly.

Again, the boys always seemed to know the prices of
everything, and would advise me very strongly as to where
things should be bought. Paper and ball-point pens, for
example, were always bought at a rather scruffy Jewish
shop up the road which specialized in cheap, slightly
soiled or damaged stuff. Rumour - through the boys - had
it that some of it must be stolen, since it was so cheap.
Cheap it certainly was, but for most of the items
concerned it was still a question of a very small price
difference.

Having been trained rather to think that price
differences are not important unless they are substantial,
and that the trouble of looking for the very cheapest
commodity is seldom worth the saving, I found this
insistence on always buying the cheapest goods almost
embarrassing. It was not that, to me, prices did not
matter, but here it seemed to have become a moral rather
than a practical question, (2) and this struck me as very
much part of the 'petit-bourgeois' syndrome I had been
accustomed to despise.

Obviously, all this was not just the boys' individual
attitude. It seemed to be part of 'the culture'. (3)
The boys, then, had certainly been trained by their
parents in this extreme respect for the worth of money
and in the logic of the market-place. It seems convenient,
therefore, to turn now to the adults of the community, and
to what I perceived as 'petit-bourgeois' and still see as
manifestations of a 'merchant ideology' in their behaviour.
Men come first in this society; I shall discuss the women
later.

Not only did Anilbhai offer me accommodation, he also helped me by introducing me to his friends. I do think that by reason of my being quite a 'novelty' - a weird foreigner trying to learn Gujarati - I also figured as something of a social asset to him, since I was his lodger and dependant. I shall return to this point about dependence, for I think it important, and it was part of my 'cultural shock' too. But first let me try to describe what happened when we went visiting.

We would travel to our destination by tube or bus - usually on a Sunday afternoon. Later, we went by car, as my landlord bought a red Mini; (4) but at first we would walk to the station or bus-stop, the man first, followed by his dependant (me) and finally the wife. This was a pattern followed by most Indians going visiting, it seemed, for the same configuration could be encountered all over north London on Sundays.

Walking first here was clearly an idiom of rank. For the man, it was then possible to set the pace, walking briskly and turning round impatiently to shout 'Come on' or something of the sort. Naturally the woman would walk more slowly, hemmed in as she was by the sari, and she would sometimes make a point of defying the husband's authority by patiently trotting along, apparently taking no notice of the shouting. But she would never answer back.

So we would arrive at someone's house, perhaps another terraced house in another Victorian street. The greeting would always make us feel welcome, whether we were expected or not. But the man would always greet us first. He was the host. It might be done more or less formally, with a full namaskar, (5) or even - sometimes - with an almost English greeting.

Tea and biscuits or Indian sweets would be served. The front room would always be used at this stage, and everyone would be seated there. I, as the most 'foreign' guest, might be given the best chair; or it might be given to my landlord, heading 'our party'; or, in some cases, the man might retain it for himself. The selection between the second and third choices clearly depended on the relative ranking of the host and my landlord. In our house, this was definitely the case, and only in a few cases did my landlord leave his usual seat for a guest. Most notably this happened when his former landlord, who was also a Desai Brahmin, visited us.

The women would sit down with us in the front room, initially, listening to the men's conversation or carrying on unobtrusive side conversations of their own. But after a while they would usually retire to the kitchen or the

back room. All the women would go and help in the
kitchen whenever any cooked food was being prepared.
I do not know, consequently, what women talk about
when on their own. But my impression, gained largely
from the subsidiary conversations carried on in the men's
presence, is that the subject of conversation is the kind
of small-talk about household matters, the family and so
on, that is heard among women everywhere.

The men talked about business. It seemed to be the
correct practice to introduce yourself, if you were not
already close friends, by giving a short summary of your
career – as you wanted it to be told. Plans, too, might
be talked about even at this introductory stage. This
kind of introduction to having a chat seemed to me, as
an outsider, almost like a ritual.

From then on people would talk about plans, plans, and
more plans; all of them connected with business. Thus
during one visit, a man lit his cigarette with a new
lighter. Closing it, he remarked: 'This is a new type
of lighter. It is very simple. In fact I thought about
going into business making it. It is the sort of thing
that could be made in Gujarat, in a small factory. If I
get enough capital I plan to do that.'

Everyone else then tried to say something perceptive
about this. What about buyers – would the lighter sell
in India? Might it not become an export article? How
much capital would be needed? And so it went on and on,
until the theme was well exploited and a new business
idea was put forward. Thus, in this particular case, the
talk about capital turned to forms of capital, to the
value of gold, and to ways of obtaining it. The host,
who had shown us the lighter, went to a cupboard and
produced a box full of gold watches. 'I brought these
from the Continent. I am going to use them as part of
the dowry for my daughters. Gold is good, but these days
gold watches are even better.' And while some of those
present might doubt the acceptability of gold watches as
part of the dowry, everybody admired the skill and
initiative involved in getting these watches through the
Customs – in fact smuggling them from the Continent.

As new business plans came up, the discussion going
on and on, it seemed to me clear that a man's prestige
was very definitely connected with the wealth of ideas
he was able to put forward during such talks. To be able
to talk intelligently about business, showing initiative
and enterprise, was the way of presenting a self to the
audience (Goffman, 1959, passim) which would gain
immediate respect. I did meet people who, lacking
interest, disappointed or disillusioned, would refrain

from taking much part in such discussions. Such people were treated with the disrespect and amused tolerance usually reserved for no-goods or nitwits.

It was from impressions such as these that my idea of the 'merchant ideology' was formed. But there was one more factor involved: if people talked about their own group as 'we Indians', it tended to be in terms of an identification with business. The African experience of the Patidars (e.g. Morris, 1968, esp. pp.91-103; Pocock, 1957a, 1957b) was obviously of considerable importance, but I do not think it the main point. The position attained by their caste-fellows in East Africa seemed to be regarded by London Patidars as proof that Indians were, as they said, businessmen: but they would have claimed that this characteristic existed prior to the African experience.

This identification with business is, it seems, something typical of Gujaratis, while not usual among Punjabis. (6) I shall return later to this aspect of Gujarati culture. Here, I should like to add that I did not find this attitude as strongly in evidence among the people of the Kanbi and Lohana caste in Coventry, where I did a short comparative study later (Tambs-Lyche, 1975) as among the Patidars in London.

This caste distinction is important. There is no 'caste system' operating in Britain, but it is at least true of the Patidars from Charottar with whom I worked in London that they have little to do with other castes. They do keep in contact with some Banias (merchant caste) and also with some Desai Brahmins, the latter a caste into which certain Patidar women can and do marry (Pocock, 1955a). I did not find that the Banias who knew my Patidar informants differed from them significantly as regards manifestations of the 'merchant ideology'. That people did not only talk business but engaged in it also, is, I think, clear from the chapters that follow.

Returning to my 'cultural shock', I was simply taken aback, I think, by the value attached to 'making money'. I suspect that my own view of money is rather one-sidedly focused on consumption: here there was a norm making it a duty to make money. Other activities were regarded as fairly useless, so to be a good man in the eyes of one's fellows was to be a good businessman. It was difficult not to think of Weber's 'spirit of capitalism' (Weber, 1930, pp.47-92).

This was bound to 'shock' a rather academically oriented socialist, not because he was unaware of the existence of such ideologies but rather because of his value-laden attitudes to them and because he did not have to live with it in his private life.

But the stress put upon money-making was only one
aspect of the 'shock'. The other had to do with dependence,
with rank, with the fundamental idea that people may in
fact be 'created unequal'. I have found no better
theoretical statement of this cultural phenomenon as
manifested in Indian society than that put forward by
Louis Dumont (1966, pp.25-30). I shall return to that
later. Here I shall just try to describe how it felt to
meet it, coming from the very egalitarian forms of interaction characteristic of Norwegian society.

My first experience of this was in the relationship
with my landlord. I have explained how we became
acquainted. I was taken under his wing, being treated
like and in fact feeling like a member of the family. But
there is more to being a father than just friendliness.
In the beginning, as had been my habit in Norwegian social
situations, I spoke to and treated him as an equal,
resenting the way he seemed to 'patronize' me when we
were visiting or attending 'functions'. (7) But I soon
came to realize that this patronizing was part of the
deal. In return for what he did for me, it was expected
that I should acknowledge, in the presence of others, that
I was, in fact, his dependant. For a long time I tried
to analyse this dependence in terms of specific relationships (landlord-lodger, etc.), and surely there are such
specific relationships involving dependence; this will be
clear from what I shall say later on. But the fundamentals
of this transaction - help, advice, even protection, in
return for an acknowledgment of dependence - are much more
general. It seems to me that this is the formula for close
personal relationships in the community. From such
'unequal' relationships groups are formed. This is in
strong contrast to Norwegian society, where there is a
tendency to codify even distinctly unequal relationships
in egalitarian terms (e.g. Barnes, 1954).

At times, then, I was inwardly burning with furious
resentment that I should be treated as a minor or inferior.
And as I was soon to discover, it was not only my landlord
who treated me in this way. Only people of very low rank -
i.e. mainly young people - treated me as an equal, or,
frequently, as somebody ranking higher than themselves.
There were a few exceptions: for instance people like
Tusharbhai (see case 2, p. 82), and the 'top leader'
himself (see p. 76) who were part of an 'intellectual
upper-middle-class' grouping which does exist in London
but which I did not study intensively. They seemed to
classify me as a research social scientist (very gratifying
indeed!) rather than just a confused young foreigner whom
so-and-so had taken into his household. Still, within the

immigrant community I had to be content with the rank
assigned to me by most of its members, and in the
beginning I felt rather snubbed.

During visits, I soon found that I was not the only
one treated in this way. In fact, conversation tended to
be shaped very clearly by differentials in the rank of the
participants. Of any two people, one always seemed to be
the top dog. When business was being discussed in the
manner described above, anyone - at least any man - could
put forward proposals; but they would always be evaluated
rather than discussed, and somebody always had a right to
the last word. He might also be doing most of the talking,
but not necessarily. He might in fact just smile and with
a short, penetrating remark make us all understand that he
was the one who really knew.

Discussions, where people disagreed and nobody could
say the final word with any clear-cut authority, were
indeed scarce. In fact I can remember this kind of
discussion only when I myself or a couple of Ismaili
students, sometime lodgers in the house, were involved.
This attribute of Indian discussions has been commented
upon by Naipaul (1964).

I think that this, too, is basic to the culture, and
certainly related to the 'fundamental inequality of man'
or 'homo hierarchicus', to use Dumont's term (1966,
passim).

I now return to my landlord's wife, and to Patidar
women in general. She was, for fairly obvious reasons,
the only woman with whom I was on close terms, being, as
she herself said, in the place of a mother to me. Her
ideas of the world and of society seemed to differ greatly
from those of the men. She would stress that 'money is
not everything' to the extent of complaining to me about
her husband's preoccupation with it. She would argue that
money is not the main prerequisite for being a good man;
that this is a moral and behavioural quality, having to do
with being 'nice', not shouting, having a steady temper,
and so on.

Religion is very much the woman's domain in the London
Patidar households. She may for example fast every Friday.
Here are the reasons my landlord and his wife each gave
for this fast:

Anilbhai's wife Veenabai: 'I fast for the good of the
family, of my husband, that he will be in good humour.'
I asked: 'So you fast, but this benefits the whole family?'
'Yes.' 'Only the women can do the fasting?' 'Yes.' Here
Anilbhai himself commented: 'Only the women can do the
fasting. I work, you see, so I cannot do the fasting.
She is the only one in the family who can do it, you see,

and somebody has to do it. It's for the good of the
family. Every Friday, my wife, she does this. It has to
do with religion, see?'
    Rank, too, plays a lesser role in the woman's world.
I did not see women in the same marital status treat each
other in the same ranked manner as the men: in fact, even
when there were substantial age differences, the impression
was one of more equality than among men. I am, however,
quite aware that there are certain specific kinship
relations where a considerable difference in rank is
recognized and is made relevant for the forms of interaction. In a sense, I believe the crucial factor to be
that a woman cannot have a dependant in the way men can,
because most of what is given in return for acknowledged
dependence is just not available to women. Thus, lacking
the resources to enter into these relationships, women
cannot become patrons, and consequently this kind of rank
difference is absent among them.
    In this introductory chapter, I have tried to describe
elements of the evaluations of London Patidars as I
perceived them. By doing this I hope to have given the
reader some idea of those impressions which have given
this book its outline and its main theme. The method
followed in fieldwork of this kind is technically very
simple, but the interpretation of the fieldworker's
experience is by no means so. Personal background and
prejudice on the one hand, confronted with the experiences
of fieldwork on the other, merge into an idea which he
then sets out to test by new experience. While the idea
may thus be strongly modified, it remains the point of
departure. Even if built upon 'mere impression' this
original idea guides and limits the work.
    Following the Myrdals (G. Myrdal, 1964, pp.xxvii-xxix;
J. Myrdal, 1967, preface), therefore, I have tried to
present these initial impressions in the light of my own
background and experience. It remains to test these
impressions, and to follow up some of the implications to
which they give rise. In order to do this, it is necessary
to define both the problem and the tools I propose to use.
That is the subject of the next chapter.

1 The problem

In this study I am concerned with a community (1) whose situation can be described briefly as follows:
1. Its members are living in Britain. The area in which they live is controlled by the state organization of the United Kingdom. 2. They work for the most part for British employers. 3. Yet they maintain a distinct ethnic identity and very largely 'keep themselves to themselves', staying away from much of the social life going on among the British. How is such a situation maintained? There exists quite a rich vocabulary of terms to describe this kind of situation, but most of these have remained purely descriptive.

One of these terms is 'minority', as defined by Wagley and Harris (1964, p. 10):

1. Minorities have special physical or cultural traits which are held in low esteem by dominant segments of the society.
2. Minorities are subordinate segments of complex state societies.
3. Minorities are self-conscious units bound together by the special traits which their members share and by the special disabilities which these bring.
4. Membership in a minority is transmitted by a rule of descent which is capable of affiliating succeeding generations even in the absence of readily apparent special cultural or physical traits.
5. Minority people by choice or necessity tend to marry within the group.

It will be seen that this use of the concept remains descriptive. A given situation can be compared, point by point, with this definition, and can then be included in or excluded from the category, as the case may be.

There is only one point where it seems doubtful whether the London Patidars fit into the category. That is Wagley

and Harris's point 3, which seems to imply that the special
traits shared by the minority's members bring, by definition, disabilities in their adjustment to the society as
a whole. In many ways, London Patidars seem to be doing
quite well, and the 'special traits' shared by the members
seem, at least not a priori, to bring disabilities only.
To decide, then, whether point 3 fits the situation I am
describing, seems to depend upon further analysis; it may
also depend upon how the definition is interpreted.

It is difficult, therefore, to use this definition as
my starting point; and since the definition remains
descriptive, it would aid classification rather than
explanation. And it is to find some kind of explanation
of the way Patidars have adapted themselves to their new
environment that is my prime concern.

The paired terms 'immigrant society' and 'host society'
may look more attractive from this point of view. They
lead one to focus on immigration as a process and open
the way to historical explanation. No one would deny the
usefulness of such an explanation. But it is with
theoretical understanding rather than historical explanation (Radcliffe-Brown, 1952, p.3) that I am concerned.
In choosing fieldwork as one's method, also, one naturally
comes to concentrate upon the kind of understanding that
emerges from what is observed during a relatively brief
period. In observing what is going on in the society
studied at any given time, therefore, one is trying to
make sense of what can be observed at that time. It may
then be held that all factors producing the situation
observed at any given moment must themselves be observable
at that moment (Barth, 1972b, p.1). Thus there is a
synchronic as well as a diachronic approach to understanding social life, stressing the timeless rather than
the contemporary in comparing social data (ibid.).

Banton, in discussing the 'immigrant perspective',
shows how timeless parameters may also be derived from
this approach (1967, p.369):

> Any host society demands certain standards of new-
> comers before it accepts them. If the standards are
> set too high, the newcomers do not place much value
> upon the acceptance accorded them. Yet if the
> standards are set very high, but still within reach,
> and the rewards of acceptance kept proportionately
> attractive, then those who win acceptance will take
> over the values of the social system and its norms
> concerning mobility will be perpetuated.

This, clearly, is a way of looking at the problem
which goes beyond description into an understanding of
important factors in the situation. It is synchronic

because the key terms are timeless ('standards', 'acceptance'). But when I tried to apply this approach to my data, I ran into difficulties. Focusing as it does on the 'standards of acceptance' of the 'host society', it suggests the host society rather than the immigrants as the prime object of study. I lived among the immigrants and had to start at the other end.

More generally, neither 'standards' nor 'acceptance' are terms easy to define operationally. And the approach seems to take it for granted that acceptance is sought by the immigrants: if we ask why, we realize that such motives may vary widely between immigrant societies. And the possibility presents itself that the members of some may have interests that are not furthered by being accepted into the fold of the host society.

Banton does himself point out the underlying assumption of a tendency to assimilation inherent in the immigration perspective. 'In general, there are grounds for thinking that, since the middle of the 1950s, the immigration perspective has become less appropriate to studies of the British scene and the racial one more so' (1967, p.384). He does not, however, define the 'racial perspective' beyond stating that its proponents believe 'that the position and prospects of coloured immigrants in Britain depend more on their being coloured than on their being immigrants' (p.384).

A more precise formulation of this approach is made by Rex. (2) He is trying to demarcate the subject in such a way as to fit a body of general theories about society. It is explicitly intended to show that within general sociology, there is 'a distinct group of social phenomena, with demonstrably different attributes from other phenomena (e.g. class), which phenomena, then, form the basis of a special sociology of race relations' (1970, p.7).

The primary characteristic of this formulation, therefore, for our purposes, is its descriptive and classificatory character. Like Wagley and Harris's definition of 'minority' it does not offer an implicit sequential approach which would enable us to see the specific racial or minority situation observed here as a product, and one of many specific products, of a clearly defined process. If such an approach is found, then the different possible situations of total integration, racial conflict, pluralism or complete avoidance could be seen as specific outcomes of the same process, having been influenced differently by certain specific variable factors in the process.

The distinction between such a 'generative' and a

'typological' approach has been made very clearly by
Barth (1966, pp.22-3):

 The differences between comparisons based on models
 of form and those based on models of process are as
 follows: a model of form is a pattern which describes
 major features of the empirical units under study.
 Several such patterns may be laid out side by side,
 and the comparison consists of noting differences, and
 discovering possible consistencies in the correlation
 of various aspects of these differences. Such a
 discovery may either be used to falsify previous
 hypotheses about the interconnectedness between these
 aspects, or to suggest new hypotheses about such
 connections.
   A model of process, on the other hand, consists of
 a set of factors which by specified operations
 generates forms. Through changes in one or several of
 these factors, different forms may be generated by the
 model.

Such a model, however, clearly needs to be based upon
some clear formulation as to the mechanisms generating
these forms. This Barth does (1966, p.1). Introducing
his model, he writes:

 The most simple and general model available to us is
 one of an aggregate of people exercising 'choice'
 while influenced by certain constraints and incentives.
 In such situations, statistical regularities are
 produced, yet there is no absolute compulsion or
 mechanical necessity connecting the determining factors
 with the resultant patterns; the connection depends on
 human dispositions to evaluate and anticipate. Nor
 can the behaviour of any one particular person be
 firmly predicted - such human conditions as inatten-
 tiveness, stupidity or contrariness will, for the
 anthropologist's purposes, be unpredictably distributed
 in the population. This is also how we subjectively
 seem to experience our own social situation. Indeed,
 once one admits that what we empirically observe is
 not 'customs' but 'cases' of human behaviour, it seems
 to me that we cannot escape the concept of choice in
 our analysis: our central problem becomes what are the
 constraints and incentives that canalize choices.
   The actor is not, of course, choosing blindly. Choice
 is made, in this model, so as to maximize value; and his
 main criterion for choice is seen to be that of obtaining
 the most, according to his evaluation, while 'investing'
 the least. This expected 'output', defined with regard
 to some highly evaluated goal as the standard, is the
 basis of the actor's choice.

Centrally in the model, therefore, is placed the actor, choosing from alternative courses of action known to him. This gives the model its dynamic quality, since a form of social process - choice - is its very core.

However, the actor need not be a single person, and frequently is not. Whereas, of course, the individual actor always makes the choice, he may do so with reference to a larger group or category of people, calculating the expected outputs to benefit, not himself as an individual, but the group or category as a whole. In some cases, the actor is free to choose his membership in the group; he may weigh the advantages of being a member against the advantages of opting out. In other cases, he is not free to choose his membership; no practical alternative is open to him or known to him, and he must act with reference to his membership as given. This makes it almost imperative for him to maximize with regard to the benefit of the group as a whole. In such cases, the group or category is obviously incorporated around an estate in Radcliffe-Brown's terms (Barth, 1966, pp.23-4; Radcliffe-Brown, 1952, p.34).

Actors clearly do not only act; they also interact, and such interaction may take the form of a transaction involving an exchange of presentations. In a transaction, both parties will obviously be trying to maximize value as seen by them respectively; they are both trying to get the maximum output. There will therefore be a tendency for the transaction to become institutionalized, i.e. the same transaction is repeated, in a form which gives to each actor the optimum outcome in the situation (Barth, 1966, pp.3-4). Clearly this does not mean that each necessarily obtains equal benefits from the transactions: this depends on the kinds of sanctions each of them has in his hands to control the other and the situation in which the transaction takes place. The similarity to economic theories about the determination of prices is clear enough. But it should be remembered that the diversity of possible sanctions is very great indeed, and that their efficiency depends on how the sanctions are seen by the recipient. Ritual sanctions can thus be very effective, even if no 'tangible' action is involved.

In this wide sense the actors can be seen as playing a game where the rules are laid down by a number of circum-stances, some of which are controlled by certain actors (e.g. military force) used as a sanction, whereas others are the result of ecological conditions such as climate or soil.

In such a model, the actor and his choice must be taken to be heuristic devices used in order to explain the relations between certain sets of facts, notably the action observed and the conditions under which it takes place. It becomes meaningless, therefore, to test whether actors actually do choose in the way described. It is certainly possible that other explanatory models may be found which at the same time provide better insight into the actor's world; why he behaves as he does. But no better model is known to me at present. And, obviously, there are a number of situations where there is no reason to doubt that the actors are really making a conscious choice of the kind depicted in the model.

When certain patterns of action recur with significant statistical frequency throughout the society studied, the society can be said to have a form, this being the aggregate result of the choices of all the actors (Barth, 1966, p.1).

When transactions occur significantly often, they may be said to be institutionalized, and they then provide a framework which may be spoken of as a transactional structure. The phenomenon described is more or less what Radcliffe-Brown describes as structure (1952, pp.188 ff.). But it will be remembered that the Radcliffe-Brownian structure resulted from norms, typified by jural norms, rather than an aggregate outcome of choices.

It will be evident that Barth's generative model has potentialities for a different kind of explanation from those inherent in sheer typologies. This model shares with Banton's exposition of the 'immigration perspective' the potential to generate different forms from the same basic process by focusing on variation in a few isolable factors. But it also has the generality that the 'immigration perspective' is lacking. I therefore propose to use Barth's model in the present exposition: what remains, now, is to apply the model to such situations as the one with which we are here concerned (see Figure 1).

From the figure it emerges clearly that there are two kinds of generating factors whose variation can be expressed in terms of the model. One is the evaluations of the actors; the other is the constraints under which the actors' choices are made.

Applying this to the kind of situation to be described here, I will remind the reader of the three characteristics that, at the beginning of the chapter, I held to be typical of the situation to be described: 1. The community's members are living in Britain, in an area politically controlled by the state organization of the United Kingdom. 2. They work mostly for British employers. 3. Yet they maintain a distinct ethnic identity and very largely 'keep themselves to themselves'.

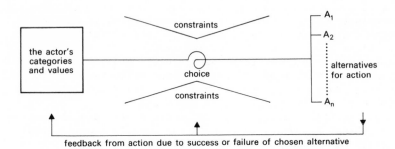

FIGURE 1   Barth's model of choice

It seems reasonable to see the insistence on separate ethnic identity as one particular instance of the variable value factor of the model. The facts of living in Britain and of working within the economic system of the host society can be seen to give rise to certain particular constraints. The model accordingly can incorporate important aspects of all the three characteristics mentioned as typical of the community studied. It remains to show how this application can be made to fit the particular circumstances. In doing this, I shall at the same time include some empirical material giving a general impression of how the Patidars' accommodation (3) to British society may be viewed. Later, I shall go on to test the emerging picture more fully in certain fields, notably economic organization, brokerage and dependence. In my conclusion, I shall return to whether these particular fields have substantiated the general idea of the relation between the Patidars and the British advanced here, and discuss some further implications.

Let me start by trying to relate the value factor of ethnicity to the model. Again I turn to Barth for a formulation which will fit my purpose. Stressing, as follows from his general model, that ethnic groups are to be seen as an outcome of social organization rather than as preconceived units on which organization is based, he points out that the maintenance of an ethnic boundary depends on dichotomization of ethnic identity in people's own categories (1969, pp.10, 14). For such dichotomization, he says, two orders of contents can be distinguished (1969, p.14):

(i) overt signals or signs - the diacritical features
that people look for and exhibit to show identity,
often such features as dress, language, house-form, or
general style of life, and (ii) basic value orientations: the standards of morality and excellence by
which performance is judged.

In the same work, Haaland, making an analysis using
this model and these concepts, has the following to say
about how the dichotomization between the sedentary Fur
and the nomadic Baggara, both living in the Darfur region
of the Sudan, is maintained (1969, pp.68-9):

The fact that the term Fur is applied to a nomad in
this context does not necessarily imply that social
situations in which he participates are structured by
the codes and values applying to a person of Fur
identity. This is the crucial criterion of ethnic
classification. If we approach ethnicity as a principle
of social organization, as a categorization defining
what can be made relevant in interaction between persons
of the same and persons of different ethnic identity.

It is in this way that I propose to use these concepts
for the London Patidars. The stress is then on the most
significant aspect: that while the London Patidars may
adopt English dress and become 'Westernized' in a number
of ways, thus to the outsider looking more and more like
the British, they still keep, for certain occasions, codes
to communicate their ethnic distinctness; and they still
judge their own behaviour and that of their caste-fellows
according to value standards that are peculiarly theirs.

But besides the 'value factor' there is the fact that
in their accommodation they are constrained by the
circumstances in which they find themselves. The economic
determinants are clearly important. As for the Patidars,
they have to fit into the industrial economy of Britain,
and this involves situations of contact where there has
to be some agreement on the definition of the situation.
The same is evidently true of the Fur and the Baggara in
their very different circumstances (Haaland, 1969, p.60):

The articulation of Fur and Baggara is thus mainly
based on the complementarity of goods and services
connected with their different subsistence patterns.
They agree on the codes and values that apply to the
situations in which they articulate whereas comprehensive differences are maintained in other sectors of
activity.

The articulation of ethnic identity is here seen as
bound up with the different means of subsistence followed
by the two peoples. These differences are maintained
because (ibid., p.61):

Fur and Baggara are categories in terms of which
actors identify themselves and their partners. Interaction is structured by a categorical dichotimization
of people who are like oneself, with whom one may have
relations covering all sectors of activity, and people
who are different from oneself, having different
evaluations, with whom one only interacts in a limited
number of capacities.

Ethnic identity is here seen as connected with the
different means of livelihood, but ultimately it is
dichotomization of identities on an ideological level
which brings about the ethnic boundary between the groups.

In principle, this applies to the Patidars in London
too. But the economic basis for the relationship between
the different ethnic groups is very different in this
case. There is certainly a 'complementarity of goods and
services' between the Patidars employed by British
industry and their employers; but the ethnic dichotomization does not follow from that relationship. Rather, the
dichotomization persists in spite of the fact that the
Patidars have to join the economic system much in the
same positions and providing much the same services as
their British colleagues. The area of contact between
the two 'societies' - the community of Patidars and
British society - is not necessarily wider; i.e. it does
not necessarily include a larger share of the social
situations in which any given individual may find himself.
But the situations of contact are determined mainly by
the British: ultimately, it is the state in Britain which
has the last word in whether the Patidars are to stay in
the country at all. Similarly, the employers may be
dependent upon labour, and may find immigrants a necessary
addition to the labour force if they are to keep their
firms going; but they are not inclined to alter the work
organization of their factories to adjust to the newcomers'
values. Thus the Patidars have to take the jobs they can
get, as well as the other contact situations open to them,
to a very large extent as given. While it is a matter of
choice to what extent contacts outside work should be
indulged in, the jobs are necessary for subsistence, and
in accommodating to the economic system of British society,
therefore, the Patidars are in a position to 'take it or
leave it'.

It is clear, therefore, that the constraints on the
actors' choices in this situation are rather different
from those of the Fur-Baggara one. These differences may
be seen to originate from the relative size and power of
the parties involved, as well as from the fact that we
have here a relation between a host society (thus estab-

lished in the area and controlling it) and an immigrant society (new to the area and therefore having to adjust to those people or peoples already there). How can the character of this specific kind of constraint be made clear?

I shall distinguish three types of constraints: cognitive, interactional and environmental. Similar distinctions are largely implicit in the works of Barth and others sharing his main approach, and have been made more or less explicitly in lectures at the Department of Social Anthropology in Bergen. I therefore do not claim this distinction as my own, but cannot find any published source to which the reader may refer.

Cognitive constraints concern the actor's knowledge of the situation in which he finds himself, and his interpretation of it. It is clear that some scientific discoveries, for example, constitute significant changes in the way certain situations are viewed by the actor, and may suggest to him alternative courses of action not realized till then.

Environmental constraints, on the other hand, can be seen to be set by the environment. The fact that a desert may not be crossed without some techniques for water supply is an obvious case. But, clearly, the amount of knowledge, in this case the techniques, which the actor can use, determines how the influence of the environment is to make itself felt.

The distinguishing feature, therefore, of environmental constraints is not so much in the fact that they are derived from the environment as in the particular way in which they influence the strategies of the actors.

Interactional constraints, finally, are constraints which result from interaction with other people. The main difference is therefore to be found in the different ways in which the 'environment' and 'other people' react to the strategies.

What is peculiar about the environment, in this perspective, is that it does not answer strategies with counter-strategies. The sea may be unpredictable; if so, no amount of strategy will make the sea answer to the actions of men by becoming predictable. What men can do is to produce strategies for predicting what the sea is up to: by modern weather forecasts this is, to some extent, possible. While this does not change the weather nor what the sea may be doing, it makes it possible for men to predict its doings and strategize accordingly.

Habermas has, of course, discussed the possibility of interaction with nature as an alternative to an exploitation of nature based upon 'Zweckrationalität' in Weber's sense, which, he maintains, treats nature merely as an object (1968, pp.8-12). But even if such ways of dealing with the environment are found - and I do not quite understand how this is to be done - the distinction he makes between work and communication remains basically similar to the one I am making: if such ways could be found, they would in my terms enter into the realm of 'interactional' constraints, since they would then be based upon interaction with a partner 'answering' to the actor's strategies.

What is important for my theme is that environmental constraints are seen to be produced by an environment (I retain this term for lack of a better one) which can be manipulated, relating to which strategies can be formed, but which does not answer these with counter-strategies.

It will already be clear what is seen as distinctive of interactional constraints; namely, that they do in fact consist of counter-strategies. Such constraints may manifest themselves not only in single sanctions. The whole strategic situation, viewed as a game, may structure the social process in such a way that certain courses of action become almost a necessity for survival, the costs of alternative action being too great in terms of the values the actors are trying to realize in the game. An analysis of Swat politics in these terms has been made by Barth (1959, passim).

The point I am trying to make is well stated by Brox (1972, pp.68-9, my translation):

If, some years ago, one came to a Newfoundland fishing village and asked why there were only small boats beached, one would get the local explanation that 'the north-west winds' (author's emphasis) made bigger boats impossible. Now it is much more likely that the answer would be that it is the fault of the government, as it has not built a mole.

What has happened, then, is that people cognitively have transferred one of the constraints they are under from the sphere of 'nature' to that of 'politics'. What was 'given' has become open to manipulation, and to abolish the constraint in question has come to lie within the realm of what is possible. It is clear that it is on this level that a discussion about the research concerning this problem has to be conducted.

Thus it can plausibly be held that people in general make a distinction between interactional and environmental constraints. But it is clear, also, that it cannot be determined a priori how or where such a distinction is drawn in any empirical case. If a technology based on 'interaction' in Habermas's terms is realized, then much

that we now perceive as constrained by 'ecology' or
'nature' may become open to manipulation (using Brox's
words). It may become constrained mainly by other actors,
by interactional constraints. If the environment is seen
as the manifestation of certain animated beings, the
relation to the environment clearly may take such a form.
Conversely, it seems clear that factors which we – from
the outside – may see as constrained by the particular
levels of cognition or by the particular kinds of social
organization peculiar to the case may be viewed by the
actors as merely 'nature'.

A question which has to be asked, therefore, if one
uses this approach is: how do the actors perceive the
borderline between environment (viewed as the aspects of
social life under environmental constraints) and interaction (viewed as the aspects of social life under interactional constraints) in the case studied? Where is the
line drawn?

Inter-ethnic relations have sometimes been viewed in
terms of ecology. They have then been looked upon as
part of the 'environment' of a given society. Such an
approach is exemplified by works by Sahlins (1961) and
Barth (1956, 1964). In these studies, interaction
between the different ethnic groups in an area is seen in
ecological terms such as 'competition', 'predatory
expansion' and 'symbiosis'. This does not exclude these
authors from seeing individuals simultaneously interacting
within the groups or across them within the region
concerned. But it seems to imply viewing, for certain
purposes, such ethnic groups as wholes having a certain
ecological relationship, as wholes, to the area and to
the other groups.

Perhaps we may go on from there to suggest that members
of such ethnic groups in contact may themselves view the
other groups concerned as part of the 'environment'.
This would imply acting towards them as if they were not
aggregates of individual actors answering strategies with
counter-strategies, but other social wholes operating
according to their own inscrutable laws. Clearly, if one
could show that such a view was in fact current among one
group's members, it would go some way towards explaining
the specific form taken by that group's relation to the
other groups.

Alternatively, people may, though belonging to different
groups, be fully aware of the 'interactional' nature of
the constraints laid upon their action by other groups.
And a quite different form of the inter-ethnic relation
may be seen to result.

The above may appear to be no more than a restatement

of the idea that roles in inter-ethnic situations may, to
a lesser or a higher degree, be characterized by ascription
rather than achievement. I hope, however, to have gone
somewhat further by relating this to a model of process.
Rex (1970, pp.144-5) has pointed out that what is involved
in these 'ascriptions' is a theory of the reasons for one
group's behaviour, as held by the other group. My
distinction between the types of constraints here may be
seen as an attempt to follow up this theme.

If we assume that such distinctions between what I
have chosen to call 'interactional' and 'environmental'
constraints upon behaviour are being made, and that they
can be applied to inter-ethnic relations as indicated,
then we can use this distinction as a 'gauge' for
'measuring' the form the particular inter-ethnic relation
is taking.

The point about using such a 'gauge' would be to make
possible comparison between e.g. different minority
communities as to 'integration'. I use this term very
tentatively, meaning the degree to which the members of
the minority interact with the majority on an 'equal'
basis, i.e. a basis where the majority is seen, by the
minority, as individuals pursuing meaningful strategies
rather than as social wholes following their own laws.
The mutual acceptance involved would be on the level of
understanding the meaning of one another's actions, e.g.
interpreting them as strategies - rather than a sharing
of norms. The contact situation is thus, in a sense,
based upon the existence of a common language of
expression through action (see Leach, 1954, p.281). It
is further suggested that this is a matter of degree,
and that this degree of common language may be one of
the most important 'variables' in the situation.

Whether, therefore, the distinction between what I
have called 'interactional' and 'environmental' constraints
is made relevant to the actors' own interpretation of the
situation is a question of empirical truth. And the
question involved is in the last resort that of an interpretation of the ideology held by the actors. Thus
cultural differences only become ethnic differences by
being expressly codified as such (Barth, 1969, pp.7-9;
Blom, 1969, p.74).

I am proposing that such a distinction can be made,
and made useful for my material. I shall try to show,
then, that the London Patidars may be said to view
British society as 'environment' - as a set of environmental rather than strategic constraints - and that this
implies a different accommodation to British society than
would otherwise have been the case. I shall then try to

connect certain aspects of the ideology of the Patidars
with their economic strategies and their relation to
British society, and attempt to demonstrate the inter-
relation of these factors.
Let me now return to the Patidars to show how this
approach will be applied. I shall, throughout the book,
refer to the London Patidars as a community encompassed
by British society. The encompassing society is then
characterized by:
1   Politically controlling its area.
2   Having a complete system of production, in that all
statuses inherent in that system are compatible with
membership of the society.
The encompassed community conversely is defined by:
1   Making use of an area politically controlled by an
encompassing society.
2   Being ecologically dependent upon niches formed by
the encompassing society, and
3   Ideologically, there is a recognition of ethnic
distinctness from the encompassing society.
This is another descriptive definition. It is,
however, my intention to show that such a situation is one
of the possible outcomes of the generative model as applied
to ethnicity - an outcome produced by the factors of
values and constraints as described above. I shall discuss
the Patidar case with this in view.
Niche in the definition above is used with the connotation given it by Barth et al. (Barth, ed., 1963, p.9).
While niche, then, is defined as part of the 'environment',
status is part of the cognitive system. It is when the
encompassing society is seen as an environment from the
point of view of a member of the encompassed community
that niche is used to denote the location from which a
means of livelihood may be extracted. This extraction, on
the level of social recognition, may crystallize into one
or several statuses. These may be seen as belonging to
the encompassed community or the encompassing society as
the case may be.
The niches, then, which provide the basis for the
encompassed community, are defined as statuses within the
system of production of the encompassing society, but for
some reason or other these statuses are not filled by
members of this society itself. The vacancy constitutes
the niche. The reason for this vacancy may be that the
status does not give a socially acceptable income
according to the standards of the encompassing society;
this is exemplified by immigrant labour in many societies.
There may be a sheer lack of personnel - as in the
seasonal migrations in Uganda (Richards, 1963; Elkan,

1960, pp.39-45) or of the Marri (Barth, 1964) - because
of religious prohibitions as the Muslim butchers of
Tibet (Harrer, 1953, p.165) - or because of lack of skill
in that particular line - as the guilds of travelling
craftsmen in the European middle ages.

Within such an encompassed community there may be -
and among the London Patidars there are - statuses based
upon the exploitation of a niche created by the members
of the encompassed community itself. The 'internal'
shopkeeper, selling mainly to other members of the
encompassed community, is a case in point. But the
secondary nature of this niche is clear: it bases itself
upon the existence of a number of customers, most of whom
are in their turn working for their livelihood in niches
defined by the encompassing society. These secondary
niches therefore do not affect the encompassed nature of
the London Patidar community.

The immigrant, then, becomes part of the British
system of production. This is a prerequisite for him to
be accepted by his 'hosts'. It cannot be altered by him.
But it would be possible for him to accept, by and large,
British patterns of consumption. If so, his ethnic
separateness would have ceased to manifest itself in this
respect, and would no longer have much relevance to his
economic behaviour. In the case of the Patidars, British
consumption patterns are not accepted. The ethnic
boundary thus has an economic significance.

Let me sum up this rather lengthy theoretical inter-
lude quite briefly. I see the ethnic boundary, in terms
of the general model taken from Barth, as a distinction
between those people with whom the actor interacts and
whose behaviour he sees as constituting interactional
constraints upon his own, and others whose behaviour he
regards as environmental constraints upon his own. The
definition describes in effect a distinction made
cognitively or ideologically by the actors. Such an
ideology, too, may or may not be chosen by the actors.
The distinction between insiders and outsiders constrains
action, in itself, to an actor taking it for granted.
It reduces the number of choices open to him. The actor
will not act in ways he does not see. The idea that
certain people are beyond the influence of one's actions,
like the wind or the sea, becomes a statement that an
action which attempts to have such influence becomes
meaningless and 'irrational'. This may have the effect
of preventing certain courses of action from being chosen.

Such a pattern would therefore tend to reproduce
itself, and might be broken only by a change in the actor's
perception of the situation. One could imagine such a

change being brought about if some empirical proof became
available that the people across the boundary might, in
fact, be influenced.

I have now slightly overstated the case: of course
ecology may also be influenced. But the way in which
this can happen remains fundamentally different from the
way in which other actors are influenced by and reciprocate one's own actions.

How, then, am I going to make use of the conclusions
reached here? First, I shall try to describe the background of the Patidars. What kind of people are they,
or were they in India? Next, Britain, conceived as an
ecological setting for the immigrants, will have to be
considered. What kinds of jobs were available? What sort
of housing? What place was there, in general, for the
immigrant in British society?

These questions might be rephrased in terms of the
model. What I try to answer might then be put as follows:
what categories and evaluations do the Patidars bring
with them into the setting? And what is the opportunity
situation facing them on arrival?

Then I will give a very brief account of the migration
itself and some aspects of its influence on the form of
the resulting settlement.

This settlement must then be described. First, I
shall try to single out the economic statuses in the
community and the transactional relations of which they
are based. I shall try to show that some of these
statuses might be said to be 'primary', in that the other
statuses are based upon transactions with incumbents of
these 'primary' statuses. These primary statuses are
based directly upon exploitation of niches formed by the
encompassing society. I hope to show that this concept
of encompassment thus becomes useful for an understanding
of the internal structure of the Patidar community.

But such statuses are ways of delimiting only certain
parts of the social process. This process is seen as the
sum of individuals acting. Next, therefore, I shall
present some cases of individual strategies. I shall try
to show how the statuses become 'stepping-stones' for the
actors in pursing their individual goals. I shall try to
show that these goals may be seen as examples of the
'merchant' ideology mentioned before.

Such strategies will be interpreted in two ways: as a
conversion of certain forms of value into other forms,
and as a succession of statuses, i.e. a succession of
relations to different people. Thus I hope to give some
impression of how individuals, in pursuing their specific
goals, come to enter into relations that result in a

certain social form.

In describing this form, I shall try to sketch the different social aggregates formed by the continuing process, such as households, temples and cultural associations.

In conclusion, I shall try to review the implications of this presentation of the data. I shall come back, then, to the theoretical points made in the present chapter and discuss their value for such a study. I shall also try to comment upon practical implications of viewing such communities as this one as 'encompassed'.

2　The Patidars' background

The strength of the merchant castes in Gujarat is common
knowledge. The Gujarati, in India, is stereotyped as the
typical businessman. Such terms as 'the Jews of India'
are often used to describe them. The Hindu merchant, as
part of the set-up of traditional Indian society, has
been described by Lamb (1939, passim). The great Gujarati
historian and man of letters, K.M. Munshi, has this to
say about Gujarat and its merchants (1954, pp.xxvi-xxvii):

These persistent activities [trading and shipping] of
the people of Gujarat through the ages led to the rise
among them of a well-to-do middle class which dominated
social life, influenced politics, laid down traditions
and shared with kings the patronage of literature.

Acquisition of wealth became an important if not
the sole end of life, and the display of it a great
virtue. The cosmopolitan spirit of this class, born
of international intercourse, did not favour an
ascetical or exclusive outlook on life, but fostered
the instinct of adaptability and catholicity of
spirit. Social inequality was based as much on wealth
as on birth and tended towards uniformity. As a
further result, life in the whole province became
dynamic. The people gained vast experience and a wide
outlook on all matters. Foreigners came to settle
among them and were in time absorbed into the
community. Neither the feudal nor the intellectual
aristocracy was powerful enough to check this endless
process of levelling and adjustment. Women waited on
masters who were neither fierce warlords nor proud
pandits, and in Southern Gujarat particularly, acquired
great freedom, sharing with men the burden of life and
exerting their influence on the environment in a manner
unknown in other provinces of India.

The soil of the mainland, watered by the rivers
Tapi, Narmada, Mahi and Sabarmati, is rich and varied,
and made agriculture a lucrative pursuit, and in years
with good rainfall gave to almost the whole of the
rural area more than enough to live on. As large
tracts were under cotton cultivation even in pre-
British days, the cotton industry flourished in towns
and villages which poured out their products into
distant lands, including Great Britain. The peasantry
consequently always has been shrewd, intelligent, and,
to some extent, cultured; and, of late, has been the
most actively politically-minded group of its kind in
the world. Till recently, prosperity through commerce,
industry and agriculture has prevented any great
disparity between the economic, religious and cultural
level of the urban and rural areas. The man of
commerce aspired to be a landlord; the agriculturalist
comes to the city or crosses the seas in search of
trade profits and on his return invests his savings in
land.

and (1954, p.ix):

Popular imagination centred around the hero of
commerce returning from foreign lands in vessels laden
with riches; around the moral and peaceful; around the
charitable, the philanthropic and the worldly wise.

I have quoted Munshi at length because his wording
provides us with more than mere facts; it also conveys a
prominent Gujarati's interpretation of them. This is not
only description of culture but certainly also stereo-
typing; and the stereotype is itself extremely significant
for our purpose.

Somewhat enthusiastic as Munshi's account may be,
therefore, it gives us a true picture of the Gujarati
national character as the Gujaratis themselves and their
neighbours like to see it.

But this must mean that Gujarat represents a regional
variation of the all-Indian 'hierarchy'. The most
insightful analysis of this hierarchy as an ideology seems
to me that of Louis Dumont. In order to make clear the
relevance of this theme for our purpose I shall have to
go into his exposition of hierarchy, albeit very quickly.

Dumont has, very vigorously, maintained that any
consideration of evaluation in Indian society should
start from the notion of hierarchy. Hierarchy he defines
as the 'principle of graduation of elements with reference
to the whole' (Dumont, 1966, p.82, my translation). The
principle of graduation of the ideology of caste is the
distinction between pure and impure; the whole is society,
in a religious sense.

There has been widespread controversy on Dumont's views (e.g. Bailey, 1959; Dumont, 1957, 1966 and 1967; de Reuck and Knight, 1966, pp.39-44). I shall not go into that here. I shall, however, draw upon his description of the ideology behind caste, stressing that I take his analysis as a description of the structure of ideology only. I shall draw on his work so far as it concerns the structuring of those values relevant for my purpose.

The overriding importance of the distinction between pure and impure will therefore be assumed. I shall assume, too, an ideological orientation towards social wholes - the kinship group, joint family, or caste, for example - rather than an orientation toward the individual. I think it is clear, from Dumont's own writings, that this is not in conflict with an emphasis on individual choice (Dumont, 1966, p.22). The individual may well choose by himself: but at the same time his choice may be made with reference to the whole group rather than himself alone. What I have in mind is that an individual may see himself as maximizing as a group member, e.g. on behalf of and with reference to the group to which he belongs.

At the apex of the hierarchy is of course the Brahmin. Sanskritization is the term Srinivas uses for groups trying to rise in the hierarchy by, by and large, imitating the Brahmins in their style of life (Srinivas, 1952, p.30; 1962, pp.42 ff). Srinivas also points out, however, that according to regional variations in the hierarchy other castes than Brahmins may come to serve as a model for emancipation among the lower castes (1962, pp.44-5). A case of conflict between the Brahmin model and the martial Rajput model is documented by Mayer from Malwa (Mayer, 1960, pp.44-5). In Gujarat, it seems, the Banias, representing the 'merchant' ideal and the Vaisya varna have come to stand in a similar position to Brahmins or Rajputs (in some places), serving as such a model for emancipation. This is commented upon by Shah and Shroff (1958, p.269).

That this merchant ideal is important in Gujarat today, is well documented by Pandit (1965, passim, but esp. p.39). In Mahuva, a small coastal town in south-eastern Sauroshtra, the big thing is to have an occupation that is 'merchant-like'. Such an occupation does not have to be commercial. The meaning of the term is close to that of 'white-collar'. Being a clerk, for example, brings to the individual high status; being a mechanic, on the other hand, gives him low prestige.

Pandit shows that this evaluation is really made relevant for the choice of occupation by the inhabitants of Mahuva. The importance of this ideal, however, does

not extend to all castes, notably not to Muslims. Hindus
excepted are the craftsman castes, who seem to value
skills higher than 'merchant-likeness'.

To sum up: it is well documented in the literature
that the merchant model is important in Gujarat society.
Its connection with the distinction pure/impure will be
fairly evident. Now let me proceed to the Patidars and
their position in Gujarat.

THE PATIDARS OF CHAROTTAR

The Kanbis are the most widely spread agricultural caste
in Gujarat. The Patidars broke off from this caste in
historic times. The process is described by Pocock (1955).
Patidar, meaning landholder, was originally a term for
some Kanbis who had become tax-collectors under the
Moguls. Under the British and the Gaekwad of Baroda they
became quite prosperous. In 1931 they insisted on being
described, in the census, as Patidars rather than Kanbis.
'This was not a sudden change, but merely the recognition
of a process' (Pocock, 1955, p.71). They have now
definitely stopped using the term Kanbi, and do not marry
their daughters to non-Patidar Kanbis (Morris, 1968, p.93).

The branch of the Kanbis from which the Patidars broke
off were the Leva Kanbis (Pocock, 1955). Geographically,
the Patidars are concentrated in the area commonly known
as Charottar, where they are dominant. This area is
roughly coincident with the administrative district of
Kaira, situated between the Mahi and Sabarmati rivers,
in central Gujarat. This area is an alluvial plain
(Spate and Learmonth, 1967, pp.650-1), and it is a good
country for agriculture. The area has generally bigger
villages than those common elsewhere in Gujarat (ibid.).
As the Patidars are the dominant caste, politically they
are masters of the local villages, and are considered to
be a rich caste.

To illustrate their position, I quote from a sample
survey of the 1961 Census of India. It comes from Ambav,
a small village of the Kaira district, dominated by
Patidars (1961 Census of India). It is predominantly
agricultural; the Patidars number 30 households out of
98. They comprise 42 per cent of the landholders, holding
71 per cent of the land. They provide 70 per cent of the
village income.

The average annual income per household of the village
was 1,927 rupees: in contrast, the Patidar households
averaged 4,332 rupees (approximately £145 and £325
respectively at the rates then current). The only Bania

family in the village earns slightly more than the Patidar average; but all other castes have an average income lower than the average for the village.

The Patidars, on average, spent 4,693 rupees per household per year, and this level of expenditure is matched by no other caste. This would have amounted to some £352 at the time. All other castes - including the single Bania family, who must be great savers - spent less than 1,700 rupees (approximately £128) on average.

If we turn to the way in which this money was spent, we find that the other castes - Banias excepted - all spent more than half their income on 'necessity' items. The Patidars used only 38.5 per cent of their income in this way.

It is necessary here to remind the reader that the sterling equivalents given are no indication of actual living standards in the village, if compared to Western countries. Their main value lies, therefore, in the relative size of income and expenditure levels as between the castes of the village. The sample survey also includes data on the distribution of some typical modern 'prestige items'. The relative 'modernity' of the caste is illustrated by the fact that 16 out of 18 bicycles, 19 out of 25 wrist-watches, 20 out of 24 carpets, 13 out of 14 wall-clocks, and 2 out of 3 radios in the village were owned by Patidars. Finally, a member of the caste owned the village's only gramophone.

This near monopoly of modern 'Westernized' status symbols contrasts with the distribution of jewellery; here the Rajputs, in comparison, have much more than one would expect from their income. As a way of conspicuous consumption, therefore, the Patidars seem to emphasize modern items, while the Rajputs stress tradition.

In the co-operative societies serving the village, most of the members are Patidars. A library and a youth club are both run by members of the caste.

I think this will suffice to show that in the village of Ambav, the Patidars are in a very strong position. Two surveys made by Dr Amin and his team of the Charottar villages of Valasan and Mogri present a similar picture (Amin 1 and 2) whereas the recent monograph by Pocock (1973) has now become the standard reference on the Patidar caste. He, too, stresses their strong position locally. Pocock's analysis, however, also points out the importance of differences in wealth and status among the Patidars of Charottar.

A short sketch of the cultural significance of these differences, as analysed by Pocock, will be needed here. As mentioned above (p. 32), the Patidars may be regarded

as a section of the Kanbi caste which has been successful
in dissociating themselves from the rest of the caste.   I
noted that Morris (1968, p.93) claims that among the
Patidars, the term Kanbi is no longer in use.   The process
of change — from Kanbi to Patidar — has also been
described by Shah and Shroff (1958, pp.268-9).   Pocock has
now given a much fuller account of the emancipation from
Kanbi to Patidar and its implications for present-day
social life.   The term 'Patidar', according to Pocock
(1973), denotes an ideal.   To be a true Patidar is not
something one simply 'is', it is an aspiration.   Thus
Pocock shows the hierarchical nature of Indian society to
penetrate the caste itself as well as the relations
between castes.   Thus, somewhat simplistically, personal
rank within the Patidar caste depends on how much of a
true Patidar one is.

Here it is relevant to see how the ideology of Patidar
emancipation fits into the merchant ideology I have
mentioned.   It is necessary, I believe, to outline briefly
how the Sanskritic idea of a four-caste society has been
used by the Patidars in this context (Pocock, 1955 and
1973; Shah and Shroff, 1958).

The Sanskritic model of society sees it as made up of
four 'castes' or varnas: the Brahmins or priests; the
Kshatriyas, comprising kings and warriors; the Vaishyas,
comprising agriculturalists and traders, and the Shudras,
the common people.   They are usually regarded to be of
descending rank, in the order mentioned (e.g. Basham,
1954, pp.137-46).   At present, a Vaishya has come to mean
a merchant.

Today, and in the two previous centuries, the main
importance of this model seems to have been to furnish a
framework for argument in the constant competition for
rank as between castes.   Today's castes, then, are not
the varnas of this classical model, but may be classed as
belonging to one or another of them.

According to this traditional ranking system, the
Patidars, when starting to rise to power as tax-collectors,
claimed equality with the Rajputs, who had previously
dominated the area.   The Rajputs, as a martial caste, are
recognized as Kshatriyas.   The Patidars thus originally
claimed Kshatriya status also.   Times were changing,
however, and according to Shah (1961), the adoption of
cash-cropping of indigo by them in the nineteenth century
led them into closer contacts with the merchants of the
area.   I have noted above the prestige that the merchant
occupation holds in this particular region (p.29).   What
could be more natural, then, but that the Patidars should
begin to claim equality with the merchants?   This, however,

implied the strange situation that they were now claiming
Vaishya rather than Kshatriya status, thus - according to
the Sanskritic model - climbing one step down the ladder
of the classical hierarchy in their claims (Pocock, 1973;
Shah, 1961; Shah and Shroff, 1958).

The Patidars have been largely successful in these
claims, and for all practical purposes they are now
regarded as equal to the Banias in rank in Charottar.
'A few Banias still insist that they cannot take food
from Patidars, but in the main the two castes may, when
the occasion arises, interchange food' (Pocock, 1955,
p.71).

Although traditionally the Patidars were a landowning
caste, they have recently gone in for trade and white-
collar occupations. Pocock has written about the small
'empires' of trade and agriculture combined which seem
to be typical of present-day Patidars, which may consist
of a variety of economic enterprises, such as pumps,
selling water for irrigation, moneylending, an oil agency,
etc. (Pocock, 1957a, pp.301-4). Such family 'empires'
play a considerable part in structuring emigration from
Charottar and resettlement elsewhere, as we shall see.

THE PATIDARS AND MIGRATION

I mentioned in my introduction that Anilbhai's father had
gone to Fiji after the First World War, to set himself up
as a businessman there. Fiji, at that time, had already
received many of the south Indian migrants that now form
roughly half its population (Mayer, 1963, p.4). It is
typical of the emigration from Gujarat that it has not
to any great extent included the indentured labour that
formed the main part of Indian migration to Fiji, or to
the other sugar-producing areas of the British Empire -
e.g. Guayana, Trinidad, Mauritius, etc. Instead, trade
seems to have been the base for the migration from
Gujarat. Businessmen from Gujarat seem to have been
found in several of the areas mentioned, but they went
to other areas also, East Africa being the most significant, though not the only, example. Mayer, therefore,
speaks of two distinct types of overseas Indian communities (Mayer, 1967). One is based - historically - on
indentured labour for plantations, or for other cash-
cropping systems set up by the British. The other
is based, at least originally, on trade and white-collar
work. East African Indian communities may be seen as
the archetype in this category. The present Indian
communities in Europe, such as the one described in this

book, resemble the second type, even if the large influx
of manual workers employed in European industry, changes
the picture somewhat. This development, however, has
taken place in the context of the type of community
originally based on business. The relation between
business and labour within the London Patidar community
forms part of the subject of this book. What is important
here is that, as Mayer has pointed out, these communities
have been recruited through the process known as chain
migration.

Chain migration implies that kinship and village ties
are constantly used to gain information about migration
opportunities, for help in making the passage, and for
assistance in the process of settling down in the new
country. For the communities formed, chain migration has
at least two salient implications. First, the community
established in the new country is likely to be structured
by the 'village-kin group' as Desai (1963) calls it. In
other words, there is a certain clustering of people
according to social ties already established in India.
Second, since these ties, binding emigrants in the most
diverse countries to each other and to the home country,
form an international network of relationships, communities
of this type cannot be viewed in isolation. In fact, it
may well be argued that there is no 'English' or 'German'
or 'East African' community at all, but several international communities stemming from caste, kin and village
ties at home, and interacting with each other at different
localities spread all over the world. The Patidar caste,
today, may be viewed as one such community.

For practical purposes, however, this book is about
that part of the Patidar community which has settled in
London, with occasional sidelights on the situation
elsewhere in England. For that local division of the
Patidar caste, certain other local divisions seem more
important than others. Having mentioned Fiji as just one
case of how far personal or family histories might take
one within this quite cosmopolitan community, I shall
deal here only with one other locality which far outshines
all others in importance for the London Patidars: East
Africa.

THE PATIDARS IN EAST AFRICA

It is not possible to date the beginning of Gujarati
migration to East Africa. It is not yet known to what
extent there was Indian trade along the coasts of East
Africa before the period of Arab expansion, and certainly

the question need not detain us here. Certainly, for most
of the era of Arab trade hegemony in the Indian Ocean,
there is no clear distinction between Indian and Arab
trade. As Arabs traded along the coasts of India, Indians
traded in Arabia, and so, in places like Zanzibar and
other East African ports, Indian traders must have been
part of the picture for a very long time indeed. A
certain vagueness about their importance there between
c.AD 1000 and the establishment of British rule during
the nineteenth century cannot be helped, at present,
though it is not unlikely that we shall know more about
this in a few years' time.

It is not likely, however, that Patidars had any great
part in this early trade. At that time they were still
tilling the soil for their Rajput overlords.

At the time when British rule was established in East
Africa and the interior 'opened up' towards the end of
the nineteenth century, however, the Patidars had become
owners of their farms. They had started cash-cropping
and their contacts with merchants had begun. They were
clearly amassing capital and they may - we have no very
solid material on which to base such an assumption -
have been in the process of entering trade even then.

Also, through their ties to the Gaekwar of Baroda, who
had been for some time a staunch ally of the British,
they had become a caste highly esteemed by the colonial
power for their loyalty and their capacity for hard work.

According to Pocock the famine and plague that struck
Charottar in 1899-1902 'turned ultimately to their
advantage ... drove many Kanbi to seek their living in
East Africa, where they turned to trade and became
prosperous' (Pocock, 1955, p.71).

It is important to note, however, that the Kanbis (or
Patidars) struck by the famine were people who, by now,
had been in contact with the market and a cash economy
for at least half a century, and that trade was a highly
respected activity. It is also important to note that,
to Gujaratis having connections with trade, East Africa
at that time was by no means a completely unknown
quantity.

In 1896, a British protectorate was established over
roughly the area that was to become present-day Kenya and
Uganda. The construction of the railway to Lake Victoria,
opened in 1903, was to become a milestone in the history
of the country. The railway opened up the country to
European settlers: it was also important for the immigration of Indians.

The railway was built largely by labour recruited in
India. Most of the labourers, however, came from the

Punjab. It has long been believed that these labourers, settling down in the country, did in fact form the foundation of the East African Asian communities. Morris (1968), however, has shown this assumption to be an unfounded myth. Studying the records of the railway company, he found almost every single labourer to have returned to India when the railway was completed. It may be relevant to note that railways were still being built in India at the time, so the navvies may have found jobs closer to home a better proposition.

However, the importance of the railway should not be under-estimated. There is as yet no history available of the Indian settlement at this early period, but opportunities for trade must have increased tremendously with the opening of the railway, and the introduction of a colonial administration, from the beginning, must have meant a certain demand for clerks and other white-collar staff.

For the Patidars, the coincidence between the building of the railway and the famine already mentioned probably to a large extent explains their position within what was later to be called the East African Asian community.

Thus the Patidars became one of the biggest communities of Indians in East Africa. They were by far the biggest Hindu grouping (Morris, 1968, pp.91ff). They concentrated on trade and white-collar occupations. Thus, in effect, in East Africa they realized the merchant ideal of Gujarati culture to a much greater extent than in Charottar itself. It is likely, in fact, that the opportunities they encountered in East Africa influenced and remoulded these ideas as held by the people back home.

I think it is fair to say, then, that the Patidars in East Africa, having become 'more true Patidar' than their relatives at home, in their turn influenced the whole idea of what a 'true Patidar' should be. I think that it is here, above all, that the importance of East Africa for the Patidars, viewed as an international community, lies.

As for the London Patidars, as we shall see, many of them came to Britain from East Africa. The importance of this fact will be discussed shortly. Even more important, however, may be the part the East African community has played in establishing that cultural identity today recognized by all Patidars as theirs.

EAST AFRICANS AND INDIANS IN LONDON

Of my informants, about two-thirds came from East Africa.

The rest may be said to have come directly from India.
As will have been made clear already, this did not imply
that they came from very different backgrounds. Those
coming from India would often have relatives or friends
in East Africa: all of them knew something of East Africa
and the situation there. Among those coming from East
Africa, all had connections in India, and when asked about
their 'home place', most would name a village in Charottar.
This applied even to people who themselves had never seen
India.

Thus the importance of distinguishing between 'Africans'
and 'Indians', as the groups were sometimes called, could
well be overestimated. Among Patidars the difference was
not often made explicit. In another publication (Tambs-
Lyche, 1975) I have noted the difference between the
Coventry and Rugby Gujarati communities, where this
distinction was of considerable importance, and the
London Patidars, among whom it has no real significance.
I then analysed the difference as being probably due to
differences in scale. It should be noted, however, than
an alternative hypothesis might be that caste solidarity
is exceptionally strong among the Patidars, who are almost
absent from the Coventry or Rugby scene. A test case
would be the Patidar community of Leicester, but I have
not personally studied this community, nor has any such
study, to my knowledge, been published.

Granted that the 'Africans' do not form a separate
group among the London Patidars, there are still some
important differences in their background, which should
be briefly treated here.

In East Africa, the Patidars were educated within the
British rather than the Indian system, and this gave them
a marginal advantage in Britain. Also, in general, people
coming from East Africa arrived in England with more money
than those coming directly from India (see also Rex and
Moore, 1967, p.131). Desai (1963, p.13) states that most
East African Indians came to Britain after 1960, and this
fits well with my own observations. There seems to have
been a wave of well-to-do Indians from East Africa
especially between 1960 and 1966. After that, the
'exodus' - always referred to as such - began. I shall
go into these matters more fully below.

In East Africa the caste system did not function as a
whole (Pocock, 1957c), but the notion of inequality,
which Pocock has termed 'difference', remained. On the
other hand, caste associations (samaj) grew up, and there
were three such associations of Patidars in 1957-8
(Morris, 1968, p.100). I came across no Patidar association of this type in London, though some cultural organiza-

tions did have a heavy membership bias towards Patidars -
notably that of Mukundbhai.

The 'Africans', in short, may be said to have acquired
through their African experience certain organizational
techniques for cultural survival as a minority. These
techniques may explain why many of them have been
prominent within the community in London and in England
generally. Among other Gujarati groups, this factor is
probably even more important, with the result that formal
organization in England among them has largely been a
prerequisite of the 'Africans' (see Tambs-Lyche, 1975,
p.350).

THE 'EXODUS' FROM EAST AFRICA

So far, I have treated 'East Africa' as one contiguous
area, since it was largely viewed in this way by my
informants. This does not mean that differences between
the situation in Kenya, Uganda and Tanzania were not
important in 1970. The 'East African Asian community' as
a whole, however, and the Patidar community within it,
had largely developed in the same way in Kenya and
Uganda. The jobs held by members of the community and
the cultural adaptations made were, as far as can be
found from the data available, essentially similar. To
a lesser extent this applies to Tanzania, since that
country, ruled by the Germans until after the First World
War, has always had a proportionally smaller contingent
of 'Asians' than the other two countries. Even here,
however, the adaptation and the structure of the
communities do not seem to have differed greatly.

Colonial rule had offered an opportunity for trade as
well as white-collar occupations to these communities.
While some members proposed to create important businesses
or to establish themselves in relatively high administrative posts, others remained at a lower-middle-class level
as clerks or rural shopkeepers. When independence became
a real possibility, several people with some capital and
close to the political scene prepared themselves for a
move. Britain, still in the early 1960s a country of
considerable opportunities, was the obvious choice. They
held British passports, identified with British rule, and
Britain itself was still open to Commonwealth immigrants.

Thus from about 1960 onwards, there was a certain
amount of migration to Britain from East Africa. As
independence came and African majority rule became an
established fact, all three countries presented the Asians,
who were still British citizens, with an ultimatum. Either

they were to become citizens of the new states or they would have to leave the country. The trickle of migrants now increased to a steady flow, hastened by the threat of new legislation in Britain, which came in 1963. From then on, until Britain closed its borders in 1967, large numbers of people migrated from all the three countries.

For quite some time it was in Kenya that the situation seemed most serious for the 'Asians'. Around 1967 a considerable number were actually expelled. They were, generally speaking, those who had not applied for Kenya citizenship in time.

In Uganda the situation was less dramatic at the time. The closure of the British borders as well as the events in Kenya, however, led to a considerable flow of people to 'beat the ban'. This flow of people lasted well into 1968 and 1969, as the people who applied for entry to Britain before closure in 1967 took their time to move.

As noted above, the first immigrants from East Africa to Britain had been relatively prosperous. They possessed some capital, they were well educated, and they were fluent in English. Their arrival in England, far from being a burden to the immigrant communities, had in fact strengthened these communities considerably, especially in terms of formal organization.

The 1967 'exodus' brought a different class of people. The newcomers were those who had stuck to their jobs and their homes, being without the capital and the knowledge of the earlier group. By 1969-71, when I did my field-work, many of them were still unemployed and some still lived with friends and relatives. The capacity of the immigrant communities to absorb the newcomers was indeed amazing, but the sitution did imply hardships both on the part of the newcomers and the established immigrants.

Then, in 1972, a new blow was dealt to the 'East African Asian' communities. Idi Amin had come to power in Uganda and embarked upon a policy of 'Africanization' which was directed against all people of Asian origin – whether they had become citizens of Uganda or not. The story of their hardships is not a subject of the present book. The arrival of the Ugandans, now plain refugees bringing nothing but their clothes and a few personal belongings, presented the immigrant communities in Britain with tremendous problems, the more so since the British economy was now in a bad state.

The implications of 1972 are outside the scope of this book, since I left the field in February, 1971. Since these implications have not been seriously studied, however, I shall try to indicate, where possible, how the present analysis of the structure of one of these communi-

ties might generate hypotheses for such study. I draw
here mainly on subsequent short visits to the field, and
on my contacts with people in close contact with the
Indian communities in Britain.

A BRIEF NOTE ON KINSHIP

The most striking aspect of the kinship system of the
Patidars is their hypergamy (Pocock, 1954 and 1973).
Women, then, marry upwards in the social hierarchy, but
the system of the Patidars is rather peculiar and calls
for further comment.
    Their villages are exogamous, and some of them are
organized into marriage circles - the term used being
'gol' or circle. The six-village circle is the highest,
centring on Nadiad, the biggest town in Charottar.
Others are the five-village circle, ranking next to the
six, and the twenty-one- and twenty-seven-village circles
(Pocock, 1954; Morris, 1968, p.98).
    Marriage is allowed within the circle, but it is also
possible for men in a certain circle to marry women from
lower circles. For the father of the girl concerned,
this would mean having to pay a higher dowry, but it also
meant establishing a relation with a more prestigious
family, which reflected on the prestige of his own, as
descent is patrilineal. Further, it meant that other
daughters might also be married upward at a somewhat
smaller cost (Morris, 1968, p.96).
    To give a girl in marriage outside the marriage circle,
however, entails the father having to pay a fine laid
down by the local caste council. This is much smaller
when she is married upwards than when she is affianced to
a man from below (Pocock, 1957b, p.21). The above is
true of the twenty-six-village circle; in the six-village
circle, marrying a girl outside is strictly not allowed.
(1)
    Patidars outside Charottar regard the Charottaris of
their caste 'as a kind of aristocracy' (Pocock, 1957b) and
try to marry their daughters into Charottar villages by
paying high dowries.
    At the other end of the scale, some Patidar women of
the six-village circle marry Brahmins. This, at least,
was insisted upon by my informants, and Veenabai, Anilbhai's
wife's, sister was allegedly married to a Brahmin - a very
expensive marriage for her family. A brother-in-law of
the sister and his wife were Desai Brahmins (as the family
claimed), and corroborated this.
    Thus, the size of dowry that a father is able to provide

is extremely important both for his daughters' and for
his own lineage. Some details may be of interest.
Veenabai, whose dowry was small because of her sister's
expensive marriage, received 16,000 Rupees, which had
been left in a bank in India. One wedding I attended in
London (not very big as people remarked - 200-300 guests)
was said to involve a dowry of £1,000. This girl was
given in marriage by Rameshbhai, but she was not his
daughter. Finally, for the wedding of Tusharbhai's
sister, where - according to 'Indian Weekly' - 1,000
guests attended, and according to other eye-witnesses,
even more, and described as 'the wedding of the year' in
the above periodical, allegedly a dowry of about £5,000
was paid. Anilbhai, on another occasion, remarked that
the minimum respectable dowry would be £1,000.

Clearly, such large dowries come to occupy an important
position in the economic strategies of the actors. In
fact, the size of the dowries was sometimes given as the
explanation of the Patidars' ability to save.

In concentrating upon hypergamy and dowries I have
confined myself to those aspects of the Patidar kinship
system which are the most relevant to the discussion of
economic strategies. I shall therefore go no further
into this system, but refer the reader to Pocock and
Morris. A full list of Gujarati kinship terms is given
in Taylor (1944, Appendix). See also Pocock (1954, 1957b,
1973) and Morris (1968, pp.94-9)

I did not carry out a full study of kinship among the
London Patidars. One point, however, ought to be
mentioned: in London, whole kin groups were seldom present.
For the individual in search of kinship contacts, therefore, it seemed of greater moment that somebody was, in
a very general way, 'related' than to spell out the actual
link. In cases such as the marriage I attended, most of
the traditional roles of kin were played by substitutes,
and the way in which such substitutes were found might
form an interesting study.

People from the same village were treated as a kind of
pseudo-kin; when roughly the same age as the speaker,
they were usually referred to as 'Bhai' - brother - or
'Bahen' - sister - as the case might be. The Patidars
used such people as contacts for a number of purposes.
But I was also told once that it is not good for kin to
live too near each other. It was Veenabai who said this,
referring to some affinals who were thinking of settling
in the neighbourhood. Generally, however, kinship - in
this vague way, was important for making contacts. And
in this matter, affinal kin seemed to be quite as
important as agnates. (Affinal kin are relatives by

marriage. Agnates are lineal descendants of a common forefather, in the male line.)

3   The Patidars' opportunities in Britain

I have tried to describe something of the background of
the Patidars; who they are and some idea of their aims.
What opportunities were open to them in the country to
which they chose to migrate?

The situation confronting the immigrants on arrival
in Britain, as well as the constraints the encompassing
society laid upon them at a later date, may be viewed as
an ecology external to the Patidar community. I use the
word 'ecology' consciously to distinguish it from the use
of environment as discussed in chapter 2. Environment
was defined from the constraints it put upon a certain
group of actors who acted from their specific background.
In this chapter I am trying to survey briefly some
important niches open to immigrants on arrival, without
asking who these immigrants were. Thus it is the
'objective situation' (1) which is termed 'ecology',
while the 'environment' refers to how this situation
makes itself felt, as environmental constraints, to
actors who are members of a certain community and constrained also by cognitive and strategic factors peculiar
to that community.

In this chapter I shall try to describe Britain as an
ecology to immigrants in general. In the identification
of the kinds of niches available to the immigrants on
arrival, two different aspects of the ecological situation
are paramount: the availability of jobs, and the availability of housing.

JOBS (2)

During the 1950s the British economy generally experienced
a period of expansion. Thus the indigenous labour force
took advantage of the opportunities for advancement to

better jobs and shunned those types of work that were
either particularly unpleasant or underpaid in relation
to the standard of living expected in Britain. This
means that the demand for foreign labour, which had
existed to some extent since the war, greatly increased.

The unpopular jobs were mainly of two kinds: heavy,
unskilled work in foundries, rubber factories, and the
like, and semi-skilled but low-paid employment in
government and local authorities, notably the post office
and public transport.

These jobs are, needless to say, concentrated in urban
areas, and the heavy unskilled factory work is located in
the industrial towns. In the north, the textile industry
offered vacancies of this kind; in the Midlands, there
are many foundries; in London there is a very great
variety of industries. These three geographical areas
are the most attractive to newcomers.

Vacancies existed, then, mainly in the following
occupations:

1 Unskilled work in the Yorkshire and Lancashire
wool industry.
2 Heavy industrial work in the Midlands.
3 Unskilled work in several industries throughout the
country.
4 Municipal transport work.
5 Nursing.
6 Some lower-paid office work in the post office and
other government services.

Besides these wage-earning jobs there was always some
possibility of starting commercial enterprises of different
sorts.

Some business opportunities could be particularly
suitable for immigrants from the Indian subcontinent.
There was a small and select market among the British for
Indian food, as well as for Indian or African 'novelties'
and other goods.

Further, there were opportunities in diverse kinds of
barely legal business on the side, and some very
definitely illegal possibilities, such as exploiting the
black-money market. This was well suited for people with
good contacts both in the UK and in India or East Africa.

While there is some evidence that discrimination
against 'coloured immigrants' has been taking place, this
seems to have had the main effect not of making jobs as
such unobtainable, but of limiting the newcomers to the
kind of work mentioned above. In their reasons for taking
on or not taking on 'coloured' labour, the employers have
generally given reasons which were based upon such
strictly economic bases as efficiency, education, etc.

That such reasons have been based also on stereotypes of
the groups in question, is of course possible: but the
economic bias of the employer's reasoning seems clear.
The 'coloured' worker, then, is valued as 'labour' by
the employers. The Patidars I studied met this by an
equally businesslike attitude to the job on their side.

HOUSING

The access to housing in Britain is not easy. First,
there are simply not enough houses in the urban areas,
just as in so many countries. Second, the system of
distribution of housing is of a special nature and
deserves comment.

Rex and Moore, in their excellent work on an immigrant
area in Birmingham, also give an analysis of the British
housing system in general (1967, pp.19-41).

Three distinct organizational structures can be seen:
the privately owned housing estate, local authority
housing and private arrangements on a smaller scale.

The private housing estates were usually built many
years ago in working-class areas, the areas with which
we are mostly concerned in this work. Through the
housewives' arrangements with the rent collector,
succession to available housing within the estate is
secured for the children of already settled families.
As Young and Willmott (1962, pp.35-43) have shown, this
can be a fairly satisfactory arrangement for 'insiders'.
If you happen to be an outsider, however, it is very
difficult to break into such a system.

The local authorities have, in some towns at least,
very active schemes for building. The access to new
housing, however, must follow some sort of pre-established
priority: hence the 'waiting lists'. But the municipal
authorities often have other priority groups to look after,
too, so that even allocations from the waiting lists may
in fact make up only a small part of the total: Rex and
Moore give an example from Birmingham in 1963 (see Table
1). At that time, 45,000 families were on the waiting
lists, and 24 per cent of the total allocations went to
them. A prerequisite for these allocations was that the
family had lived in the area for at least five years -
until this condition was fulfilled, it was not possible
to get on to the waiting list at all. As for an immigrant's
chances of obtaining such housing, no further comment
should be necessary.

TABLE 1   Planned allocation of council houses in
Birmingham, 1963

Public Works Department (road-building, etc.)	472
Key workers rehoused in overspill	50
Special medical cases	170
Slum clearance	1,984
Demolitions and closing orders	490
Dangerous dwellings	20
Waiting-list allocations	1,303
Homeless families	850
Total	5,339

It is appropriate to mention here that this prerequisite
for acceptance on a waiting list was taken up by the
Institute of Race Relations (Rose et al., 1969, p.694) to
some effect. It should also be emphasized that such
restrictions are laid down by individual local authorities,
and thus differ a great deal from one area to another
over the whole relevant period. A discussion of such
differences - and of the relation of local government to
immigrant housing in general - has been made by Burney
(1967, passim, esp. pp.58-79).

Slum clearance, as emerges from the Birmingham example,
is of considerable dimensions in most industrial towns in
England. This reduces significantly the availability of
housing within the private sector, to which, it is clear,
immigrants were largely restricted. In such private
housing, then, the remaining houses became increasingly
crowded (for examples, see Rex and Moore, 1967, pp.27 ff.;
also Burney, 1967, passim; for Yorkshire, Butterworth
(ed.), 1967, pp.5-13).

However, the demand for accommodation, from both the
British and the immigrants, was such that room-letting
constituted an ecological niche for those newcomers who
had been able to buy a house (Rex and Moore, 1967, p.38;
Desai, 1963, pp.39-55).

For some of the immigrants, then, buying a house was
one of the more attractive possibilities. The three
geographical areas mentioned - London, the Midlands, and
the north - differed considerably as to prices and
availability of houses for sale. In the north, houses
might be bought very cheaply, though in some places only
the smaller type of working-class cottages were to be
found. The price could be as low as £400-£500 (Rex and
Moore, 1967, p.30, and my own informants). In the
Midlands, the situation was not very different, except

that prices were much higher. When I was in Coventry, the
price for such a house there seemed to vary between £1,500
and £2,500 (the latter, though, would buy a house in very
fair condition), and in Rugby, informants gave £1,500 as
a fairly standard price. In London, the prices were very
much higher still. The smaller type of house was not
widely available, and houses priced under £4,000 were
very scarce indeed.

In all cases, for new immigrants, loans and mortgages
were difficult to obtain. Naturally, the newcomers could
offer little security and were too recently established
to be able to produce much in the way of references from
employers and the like. At the same time, building
societies were not willing to give mortgages on very old
and very short-leased property. It is only fair to say
that the situation seemed to be improving in this respect,
and in Coventry, quite a few of my informants got a
mortgage on a council guarantee, even though their finances
were rather uncertain.

Some groups among the immigrants, and notably the
Indians, however, were able to overcome these obstacles
because of their social organization: this seems also to
have been true of the Patidars. They largely lent and
borrowed money for the purpose within the community, and
also formed partnerships for house-buying (Desai, 1963,
pp.39-55).

Immigrants, then, on arrival, had really but two
choices open to them as regards housing. If a man could
raise the necessary capital, he could buy a house.
Otherwise, lodging-house accommodation would be the only
alternative. As a variation of the first choice, he might
buy and run a lodging-house. Rex and Moore have pointed
out how lodging-house life can be seen to produce negative
attitudes to the newcomers from neighbours and others
(1967, p.265). This was especially so in the case of
inter-ethnic lodging-houses.

These three choices, influenced by the local prices
and the local availability of housing, may be said to
form the niches open to immigrants in housing.

There are two further points that should be discussed,
however briefly.

It might seem that few jobs among those mentioned
would be worth coming a long way for. But if the differences in wages between India and Britain are taken into
account, the relative attraction of Britain is obvious.
A bus conductor in London Transport earns, even in basic
wages, more than twice the salary of a university
lecturer in India. If overtime is included - as it is by
the London Patidars when they make the comparison - one

can earn three to four times more in Britain. And if we
instead compare the wages of a labourer in India and in
England, ten times as much money can be earned in Britain.
Even with living costs much higher than at home, emigration
has paid off in money terms.

The second point is quite different. I have already
noted some of the problems inherent in using the term
'ecology' for the host society. Accepting this usage,
however, what can be said about the niches offered to the
immigrants, if we look at them from the point of view of
the British?

The British clearly have established an industrial
organization which the immigrants must accept. The
society based on this industrial economy is one of class;
and the niches filled by the immigrants naturally put
them, from the point of view of the British, in the
'working class'. This is what Desai means when he says
that the immigrants are identified with the working class
(1963, p.68).

In Marx's terms, they become part of the 'class-in-
itself', but not necessarily of the 'class-for-itself'.
In Weber's terms, they become part of the working class,
but not of the status group of workers without any
specific identification of their own with this status
group (Marx, in Bottomore and Rubel (eds), p.195; Weber,
1967).

The distinction is important, as we shall see, because
the London Patidars generally see themselves very
distinctly as non-working-class. This does not seem to
be true of some other immigrant groups, notably the Irish
and the West Indians (for both groups, see Rex and Moore,
1967, pp.84-115; for the West Indians, Patterson, 1965).
I shall return to this, however, in chapter 8.

The general relegation of immigrants to the working
class by the British has, however, heavily influenced
the discussion of the 'immigration problem' in the British
press and political circles. It has tended to concentrate
the discussion on such matters as 'competition for jobs'
and 'overloading the social services'. Immigrant unemploy-
ment has been the focus of perhaps undue attention. A
polemical discussion, but well argued and documented, of
this theme is found in Foot (1965). The results of a very
extensive survey of the attitudes of the British to 'race'
is summarized in Rose et al. (1969, pp.551-604). These
attitudes may of course also be looked upon as part of
the 'ecology' for the members of the encompassed community.

4 Migration

'The first ones to go to Britain from [Anilbhai's home
town, one of the biggest towns in Charottar] were
N.P. Desai and some of his friends. There were four
of them. All were Desais - from that part of the
village. They originally booked for Borneo, to take
land tenancies and become farmers there. They got the
tenancies free, the instalments, that is, a 999 years'
lease. They would also get everything they needed on
credit. But these people said: "We will go to Borneo,
but we will go through London, and embark for Borneo
there." So when they came to London they decided there
was money to be made here. And they stopped in London
and never went to Borneo.

'That was in 1952. They were the first ones to go
to Britain from X. My father had just returned from
Fiji, in 1951. He knew the father of one of those who
had been emigrating. That was one, a Desai, a friend
of N.P. Desai. And this father, he was a tailor in
Nadiad. He and my father, they used to talk in the
evenings - you know, the old people like to sit and
chat about the old days. One day this man told my
father that his son, he had gone away to Britain; he
had not heard of him since, he had not sent any money
or anything. "I don't even know what he is doing."
My father did not know much about England, he had
never been there, he had lived all his life in Fiji,
you see. So he asked: "Is your son in England? What
is he doing there? Is he studying or something?" So
the man told him that his son had not even finished
primary education. "But what is he doing in England,
then? England is the centre of the empire!" He did
not know very much about Britain.

'I was not interested in Britain at that time. Why should I? I was nineteen years old in 1952. But in 1956 I married. My mother, she was a very nice woman, she was good. But she had had very little education, only in Gujarati, and she did not understand the modern life. So my wife and my mother did not get on well together. So there was trouble, you see?'

Comment

When Anilbhai arrived in England, he went first to Patidar village-mates in a West Yorkshire city, thus behaving according to what Price, for example, calls 'chain migration' (1963, p.85). The people, then, choose to migrate on information supplied by kin or village mates who have already left; they are helped by these when they arrive and, consequently, migrants from one place tend to cluster together in the new country. This is well suited to what Mayer calls the 're-creation' of the 'village universe' (1959, pp.11-12). Such chain migration and resulting re-creation of the village universe has been pointed out for Coventry Sikhs by Thompson (1970), for Lancashire Gujaratis by Lyons (1971, esp. p.7), and generally by Desai (1963, pp.17-18). My own observations, from the Coventry and Rugby Gujarati communities as well as from the London Patidars, are entirely in accord with this. Indeed, this has led to some British towns becoming Patidar centres, notably Leicester. Coventry, in contrast, had only two Patidar families, and there were no Patidars at all in Rugby.

As with the villages of Charottar (Pocock, 1957b), the English towns with many Patidars, who had a high general socio-economic status, were ranked high by my informants, while those with few Patidars and where other (and lower) castes formed the majority of the Gujaratis were ranked low. The kinds of work available were also important in determining the ranking of a town. But clearly no systematic hierarchy of English towns had emerged. Outside London, which was the 'highest' place in everybody's opinion, Leicester seemed a safe second. Birmingham, at the other extreme, was universally described as 'jungly' and 'low'. This, of course, does not fit too badly with common views among the English.

The mechanisms of chain migration, then, have produced a very uneven spread of Patidars in England, and have led to their concentration in certain towns. In some towns, also - Coventry is a good example (Thompson, 1970) - Patidars as well as Indians concentrate in certain areas.

In London, such concentrations are not very marked. I found Desai's statement (1963, p.20), that the Gujarati immigrants largely live in 'houses scattered in Hampstead, Kilburn and South Kensington. Some live on the north-eastern part of the North Circular Road', still true, but would add parts of South London (Streatham for example, and Croydon) and Golders Green. The last suburb is interesting because it is largely seen by the English Gentile as typically upper-middle-class Jewish, and this fact is often mentioned when immigrants say that the Gujaratis 'are becoming just like the Jews'. To move to Golders Green, however, is possible only if the immigrant has already attained a fair level of economic success.

There is, among London Patidars, no clear geographical clustering because of kin or village ties, but these ties appear very clearly, however, if one is looking at their social contacts. Families habitually have to cross large parts of London when they go visiting on Sundays. For my fieldwork, this presented some difficulty, as it meant that I had to extend my own network by being taken visiting: I could not just 'settle down in the community', and I was able to interview fewer informants on that account.

5   Statuses and relations

In this description I am going to concentrate on the
economic organization. I shall do this, by describing
first the statuses forming the framework for economic
organization; later, I shall go into, by case studies,
the strategies actors follow with reference to that
framework. Finally, I shall try to sum up briefly the
resultant form.

   In presenting the statuses, I will describe first
those which, historically, came first. The approach is,
however, evolutionary rather than historic: I am trying
to describe how the statuses that came into being later
were founded upon transactions with the incumbents of
those statuses already present. I shall be referring,
for the historic sequence, to Desai's work (1963) in
some respects but the picture of the sequence as
presented has largely come out of the case histories of
my informants. The strategies presented later, therefore, will present generally the same picture of the
processes of establishing the community. With this in
view, no separate historical exposition has been
deemed necessary.

   Looked at from this point of view, the statuses
cluster themselves conveniently into primary, secondary
and tertiary.

THE PRIMARY STATUSES

The two first statuses to be established, the worker and
the 'external' shopkeeper, have in common the fact that
their incumbents deal direct with members of the
encompassing society (Fig.2). Thus they are primary not
only in time, but also in an 'ecological' sense.

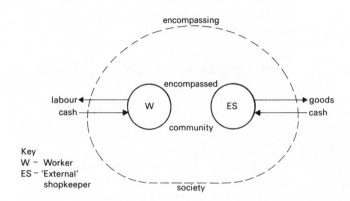

FIGURE 2   Primary economic statuses

The worker

The worker becomes part of the labour force of the
encompassing society. Thus he enters into one of the
established statuses of that society and, from the point
of view of his employer, occupies the same economic
position as any other holder of that status: he sells his
labour for a cash wage.

I must admit that I was not able to study the worker-
employer relationship directly. It was possible to find
out from my informants only what jobs they held and
their attitudes to them. Some idea of the relationship
may be obtained from written sources, but usually there
is little specification of the original nationality of
the workers, and their caste is never specified.
However, I shall try to put together as close an approxi-
mation to the real situation as possible.

These fragmentary sources do not add up to a very
satisfactory description of the relationship between
encompassing society and encompassed community as it
manifests itself in the relation between the labourer
(as member of the second) and the employer (as member of
the first). I shall do my best to write about the
relationship with reference to this framework.

What stands out, then, is that the relationship is
circumscribed by (a) the employer's total position in the
encompassing society, and (b) the employee's total
position within the encompassed community. These positions,
being total, must include affective factors not present in
the relationship between employer and employee. In
contrast to these total positions, the relationship

between the two is largely economic, involving mainly the exchange of labour for cash.

The relationship itself can of course be observed only at the place of work. The majority of the group I was studying did not work together in the same firm, but were scattered all over London in a multitude of different jobs and firms. To study them at work was therefore well-nigh impossible.

It may, however, be permissible to study the attitude of the Patidar employees to their work from employers within the encompassing society, and to focus on this. This can then be compared with what is known about the British employers' attitude to immigrant workers in general and Indian workers specifically.

What I am trying to demonstrate can be summarized as follows: (1) that the employers view this relationship as fundamentally similar to that with their workers in general; (2) that the Patidars' position within an encompassed community is relevant for their choice of and their attitude to work.

The employers clearly turn to the Patidars not for any specific reasons but as part of the available labour force. This is quite clear from the literature (Patterson, 1965, pp.77-125; McPherson and Gaitskell, 1969, passim). McPherson and Gaitskell classify the reasons employers give for rejecting 'coloured labour' as follows: (1) the other staff; (2) public/client/customers would object; (3) lack of education and experience: in this last category they include 'the over-qualified applicant'. A short interview with a manager of a small South London firm confirmed my own impression that this problem of 'over-qualification' is a very serious one for my informants. The Indians, he said, were good workers, but often did not mix well with other staff: they were inclined to regard themselves as socially 'above' the other workers. Their problem was similar, he said, to that of employees with a British middle-class background.

Though discrimination on the grounds of colour in selection for jobs is now illegal such legislation is obviously very difficult to enforce. The British way of recruiting labour relies very heavily on interviews. This makes it personal rather than formal: the impression an applicant makes during an interview becomes relatively more important than his papers and formal qualifications. In such a situation it is hardly possible to prove discrimination, since it is not possible to refer to such manifest evidence as the exams taken, the length of experience, etc. The employer can always just state that he 'preferred the other man'.

The reasons referred to by employers for not taking on
'coloured' staff may hide actual colour prejudices, but
they are phrased in a way which relates them to the
economic aspect of the relationship between employer and
employee. If the other staff react adversely to the
'coloureds', this soon becomes an economic problem for
the employer. He might risk a strike; he might risk
losing as many workers as he would gain by taking the
newcomers; he might see himself as destroying morale and
thereby reducing the relative productivity of each worker.
His refusal on these grounds may therefore be seen to be
rationalized in economic terms.

Similarly, if public, clients or customers object, he
would lose business: this is also a refusal on economic
grounds. Finally, 'lack of education and experience'
reflects quite simply a fear that the worker in question
may not be worth his pay in terms of the prevailing price
paid for labour. This, again, is an economic factor that
the employer has to bear in mind.

Whether or not there is discrimination behind these
reasons (and there may be good reason to think that it
does exist) is not the chief factor. The main point is
that this discrimination - or we may call it just
'preference' - is put across in economic terms, and that
this economic argument is consistent with the game the
employer has to play if he is to survive in the capitalist
industrial economy of the UK. However many workers the
employer needs, they have to be engaged on such terms
that he can make a profit.

Thus the employer is clearly dependent upon his general
position within the encompassing society for the transactions he wishes to make with Patidar workers.

Whereas for the employer, then, the prospective
employees seem to be viewed largely merely as labour, and
evaluated accordingly - with perhaps a dash of prejudice
thrown in - the Patidar in seeking employment seems to
see the labour market strictly as an environment out of
which he wishes to get the best deal possible. Often he
looks upon the job as just a stepping-stone to another
career. This was true of Tusharbhai before he started
his first shop; it was true of Rameshbhai during his time
in the north; it was still true of Harishbhai, as his
aspirations were clear enough: to find something in the
way of business which would give more prestige and money
than his factory work. It was true of Mr Dhruv, a lodger
in Anilbhai's house, when he worked in a provincial town
to save money for his London studies. And it was even to
some extent true of Anilbhai himself, since he was always
thinking of 'some business' on the side. Unlike many

British-born workers, he is therefore eminently mobile
(Desai has some good examples; 1963, pp.79-80) and
willing to go to great lengths generally in order to make
money.

Because of the housing arrangements - the Indian
workers lived in Indian-owned houses - and the fact that
they were everywhere welcomed by caste-fellows, fellow
villagers or relatives, they were able to move to wherever
work was available at the time. Thus, when times were bad
in Bradford, they moved to Birmingham, and vice versa.
Overtime, too, is probably much more sought-after by him
than by indigenous labour. For example, Anilbhai stated
that he always accepted overtime, and that he felt
unhappy on Sundays because there was nothing to do.
Rameshbhai made good use of overtime when he was in the
north and others also stressed the importance of overtime
(see also Desai, 1963, p.70).

The Indian students I knew had no scruples in these
circumstances about trying to make their prospective
employers believe that they would in fact settle in
England, even if they knew very well that they were going
to return home in a couple of years. This was necessary
for the individual in his maximization of resources: he
had to get a job, and could not unless he 'cheated' in
this way. But the cumulative result of such a strategy,
one suspects, must be to make employers even more wary
about taking on Indians.

Concerning Gujarati immigrants trying to find work,
one informant was one of the non-Patidar students in
Anilbhai's house. He told me: 'When I applied for a job,
I tried 250 jobs in three weeks. If I had been a European,
the jobs would have come begging.' He did also state
that one reason for his difficulties was that he could
not get any recognition in England for his experience
gained in the Sudan. He was a newly-qualified accountant.

This is a common experience. Particularly important
is the lack of recognition of previous education and
experience, which is particularly serious for those of my
informants who were educated in India. Indian university
degrees are not only seen as inferior to English degrees -
an evaluation which is, at least with only very few
exceptions, reasonable - but they are often given no
recognition at all. Thus a man who has, let us say, an
MA from India is not classed as skilled at all in England,
and has to start from the very bottom. This is obviously
unjust, and a problem of such importance for my informants
that something should be done about it. A set of official
'guidelines' for employers by which to assess Indian
educational backgrounds would be useful - in the form of

'translations' into English qualifications which might be
seen as roughly equivalent.

One aspect of the lack of recognition of Indian
education, treated also and more fully by Desai, is the
fact that many immigrants who originally came to study in
Britain have been frustrated in their attempts because no
English institution would assess their qualifications,
and have therefore given up their further education and
gone in for labour or business instead.

Even if many of my informants had settled down with
their families and thus could not move quite as freely
as before, I did come across people who worked in London,
where they rented cheap accommodation, and kept their
family in the Midlands. Harishbhai is an example of
this. The idea, of course, was to make use of the
differences in wages as well as the cost of living
between the two places. Likewise, Ashok Patel tried to
make the move away from London when he expected his
mother to join the household, so as to be able to keep a
higher housing standard.

The attitude to mobility was positive. But, at the
same time, it appeared that the general direction of
movement was from the Midlands and the north to London,
the most highly ranked city. According to the president
of the Hindu cultural association in Rugby, four out of
five of the Gujarati families who had left in the previous
five years or so had gone there.

Chain migration has restricted the number of towns
where a Patidar has friends and relatives- but these
towns are well spread out. Thus while Coventry was
almost wholly non-Patidar, there were quite a few
Patidar families in Nuneaton only a few miles away.

In London, all castes present in England can, I expect,
be found. During the early phases of migration, according
to Desai, there were quite a few Indian workers who acted
as middlemen in recruiting Indian labour or in getting
Indians a job, from whichever point they were viewed
(Desai, 1963, pp.78-82). It seemed to me perhaps because
of the kinds of jobs my informants held, that this was no
longer so. But I was also told that the position of
such middlemen had become rather less important since the
1962 Commonwealth Immigration Act, which functioned to
restrict unskilled workers from entering the country.

The Patidars are in many cases white-collar workers,
and they were often proud that there were 'no other
Indians in my firm'. This would mean that the speaker
had not needed a middleman, but had been able to make his
own way in British society. It therefore proved the man's
independence, and hence he often stressed it.

The Patidars, therefore, as employees in British society, seem interested primarily in the money and second in a white-collar occupation. The word 'clean' is often used in approval of such work. But in many cases, work for wages is only one of several sources of income, as chapter 6 will show. Thus it is important to find jobs which can be easily integrated into a general strategy aimed at economic success. Few Patidars therefore identify themselves with work for wages, so that they become 'workers' in their own eyes. They do not seem to identify at all with 'working-class culture', but remain very much oriented towards the middle class. Even when going into pubs (as some, but not many, do), the public bar was usually shunned in favour of the saloon, because, it was explained, the people in public bars were not among those with whom one would wish to associate.

It seems, then, that the employer from the encompassing society does view the Patidar worker as labour in a purely economic sense. His reasons for refusing 'coloured' labour are couched in the terms of economic rationality. As to the Patidar working for wages, he remains primarily a Patidar and is only 'incidentally' a worker, i.e. he is using the job to attain goals valued by his co-Patidars, and is not accepting the identity of 'worker' and the evaluations forming the 'working class culture' of the encompassing society.

The barrier between the encompassing society and the encompassed community, in such a situation, comes close to what Barth (1963, p.9) discusses in his work on entrepreneurs:

> The occasional need for repudiating relationships point to possible connections between entrepreneurship and factionalism or social stratification: both of these forms of social division imply limitations or discontinuities of obligation and commitment. They are thus social barriers which may give strategic scope to certain kinds of enterprise, and may even be generated by the entrepreneur where the advantages he gains (and can offer those who follow him) outweigh the costs of repudiating the relevant relationships.

Thus, the barrier created, and which I have illustrated in the accompanying diagrams, is not one between economic spheres. Such barriers exist when the goods circulating in the different spheres can be exchanged only across sphere barriers in certain strictly limited ways (Barth, 1967). In this case, on the other hand, there is a discrepancy of evaluation as between the encompassing society and the encompassed community. The barrier here also produces certain limitations on exchange, but these

are clearly of a different order from that of sphere
barriers.

The main point about encompassment is that the member
of the encompassed community regards the encompassing
society as an environment, and thus maintains attitudes
to work and work-mates differing from those of the members
of the encompassing society working in the same jobs.
This is because these jobs are seen as being part of
strategies orientated towards the values prevalent in the
encompassed community. A complete assimilation, in
Desai's sense (1963, p.147), of the Patidars would have
to imply giving up this orientation. To keep it, on the
other hand, gives the ethnic boundary much of its economic
significance.

The 'external' shopkeeper

The 'external' shopkeeper distinguishes himself from
other shopkeepers in the community by not being primarily
dependent upon the members of the encompassed community
for his customers.

Desai mentions external shopkeepers among the earliest
Indian settlers in the UK (1963, p.57). The first,
according to him, set up shop in London in 1928-9. Their
franchise was based upon Indian students, the occasional
Indian businessman or intellectual, but most of all upon
the English, among whom Indian food and spices had become
popular, notably in middle-class circles.

The earliest Indian grocers in England, therefore,
took their place beside such phenomena as the 'Continental
delicatessen' and the like, usually being situated in or
near the better areas, and selling to middle-class people.
The relationship between shopkeeper and customer, in this
situation, is purely economic, though the customers might
be very steady and on friendly terms with 'their
specialist'. It would not, however, be necessary for
such an 'external' shopkeeper to become a member of the
encompassing society; on the other hand, his commercial
activities do not in themselves place him within the
encompassed community. Prices and goods, therefore, for
such shopkeepers, remain geared to a market consisting of
British middle-class people and Indian intellectuals.
'Ordinary immigrants' are to some extent excluded from
becoming regular customers. Thus Veenabai, for example,
(my landlord's wife), would not think of ordering her
goods from Tusharbhai's shop, even though Tusharbhai was
her village-mate and their fathers knew each other well.

There are a multitude of 'external' shopkeepers in

London, and the Patidars have their share in this trade, for example, Tusharbhai's. His was a grocery and health food business, but it is important to note that there are numerous shopkeepers of this kind specializing in trades other than groceries. The many 'novelty' shops sell Indian and East African handicraft products, cloth and sarees, etc., also Indian kitchenware and different combinations of these kinds of goods, often including Gujarati and some Hindi books and newspapers. Groceries are often combined with these durables, and there is not much variation between the kinds of goods sold by 'external' and 'internal' shopkeepers. The main difference is in the price and the 'fanciness' of the goods, but there is also a tendency for the 'external' shops to be larger and more specialized. As the customers differ, so often does the style of shopkeeping. While the 'internal' shops tend to become meeting-places where Gujaratis would gather for a chat and discuss the latest news of the community, the 'externals' are often eager to prevent this and insist on a businesslike manner. The owners also differ slightly in form of speech, etc., trying to play up to English middle-class mores.

In some cases, of course, the shop combines the 'external' and the 'internal' type of business, but this is not usual. There is also a difference between those who have 'external' customers to any significant degree, and those who have practically none. In the latter, the shop might be tended by a wife who did not speak much English.

In two cases I came across shops which based themselves on a mix of customers rather different from the types indicated above. One was a Patidar grocer in the Notting Hill area of London who sold some typically Indian goods but primarily dealt in the same commodities that might be bought in an English-owned grocery. It was clear that his custom was largely based on non-Indian immigrant, notably West Indian, local residents, as not many Indians, and even fewer Patidars, lived in the area.

In Coventry, one of the leaders of the Indian community, a Patel but not a Patidar, kept a record shop specializing in West Indian as well as Indian music. Here, again, the presence of another immigrant group provided a niche for Gujarati-owned business.

These immigrant-based 'external' shopkeepers are clearly a relatively recent phenomenon as compared to other 'external' business, and cannot have had much of a niche open to them before the middle 1950s. As it is, the Coventry record shop dates from about 1962-3, and the Notting Hill shop from the late 1950s.

In all these cases, the relation between the 'external' shopkeeper and his customers remains of a business nature and a secondary relationship throughout. In some cases, customers from the encompassed community may be able to get some price reduction. But this can be done only when there are no other customers around, and is not a fundamental trait. The relationship between these business men and their customers, therefore, serve to maintain rather than to break the boundary between the encompassed community and its encompassing society. Nor does it serve, in the cases where customers come from another immigrant group, to break down the boundary between this group and the shopkeepers.

There is also external business other than shopkeeping, but I shall concentrate on the most significant economic statuses, and ignore those in which very few people engage. Moreover, other external business is not so much a status of the encompassed community as it is a case of certain of that community's members entering into positions within the encompassing society. This is true of doctors, solicitors, etc., in so far as they serve indigenous people. Unlike the 'external' shopkeepers, the fact that they are Indian is no specific asset for their business as such.

The 'external shopkeeper' is the only example of a status open to the Gujaratis purely on the basis of their ethnic identity. It is the only clear example of an ethnic division of labour between the Gujaratis and the British. This has implications for the 'image' of the Gujaratis as seen by the English; they too see Indians, to some extent, as businessmen. It is not possible to say how much this factor has influenced the 'merchant ideology' of the Patidars in Britain; yet since the 'external' shopkeepers were the first Gujaratis to 'make it' in Britain, their influence on the self-image of the present community may be quite important.

THE SECONDARY STATUSES

It is on these two primary statuses that others within the encompassed community are built; they are based on transactions with incumbents of the first two.

The statuses to be described next will therefore be termed 'secondary', and I shall distinguish five of them: houseowners; 'internal' shopkeepers; moneylenders; brokers; leaders.   The transactions between the holders of these statuses and the workers are shown in Figure 3. In these relationships, the worker enters into specific dyads for

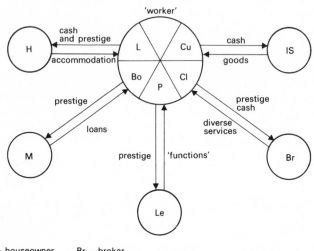

Key

H – houseowner	Br – broker
L – lodger	Cl – client
M – moneylender	IS – 'internal' shopkeeper
Bo – borrower	Cu – customer
Le – leader	
P – public	

FIGURE 3   Secondary economic statuses

specific purposes, and it is therefore convenient to
single out the part-statuses that emerge (see Figure 3).
To be correct, the 'worker' here stands for the person
rather than the status in Radcliffe-Brown's (1952) terms.

The lodger-houseowner relationship

The definition of these two statuses is, I think, fairly
obvious, but in order to give the complete picture they
must be described in view of the relationship between
them.
    When I arrived in 'my' house, the owner stressed that
he saw this relationship as essentially non-commercial:
'In this house, we are almost like a family.' He insisted
that his wife was called 'Bhabhi' -'elder brother's wife' -
by the students living in the house. This term has, in
Gujarati, also a wider pseudo-kinship meaning, rather
like the English 'Auntie'. In time, however, I found
that it was very rarely used by the lodgers. When I
myself used it at the beginning, this brought a slightly
amused smile from my co-lodgers at the dinner table - she
was usually called simply 'Mrs Patel'.

The status delineation is perhaps best illustrated by
using myself as a 'borderline case'. As already mentioned,
I spent most of two months living in the boys' room. Here
was the family's spare bed for visitors, and though I did
pay a weekly rent for it, I was repeatedly assured by Mrs
Patel that I was 'just like another son. Now I have three
sons.' They said I could have evening meals with the
family whenever I wished, including Saturdays and Sundays,
whereas the other lodgers were not allowed this privilege.
I was told that whereas the other lodgers were coming
into the lounge just a bit too much to watch TV, I should
not refrain from using it for that reason. 'This - your
house', as the incomparable Mrs Patel said. Unlike the
other lodgers, I did not even have to go out to the
laundrette with my washing, she would do it for me. At
the same time, I was described as being of 'the same
caste' as my landlord - a very flattering remark.

But this emphasis on a personal relationship did not
extend to the lodger status per se, whatever the owner's
assurances to the contrary. The lodger-owner relationship was more of a business than of a family relationship
in this case. Thus one of the students living in the
house was reported to have had a row with the owner, who
had promised to install hot water in his room, but had
failed to do so. When the lodger complained, they had a
row, ending with the owner shouting at the boy and telling
him to leave the house that very minute. But the lodger
dared him to throw him out, and finally the owner gave
in and provided the hot water.

My favoured position caused problems for me, which
involved the universal problem of protecting a backstage
where I was given advantages not offered to the others.
The owner himself was very much concerned about this,
telling me to conceal these things from the other lodgers.
This involved, for example, going to the toilet from the
lodge to camouflage my movement towards the kitchen. I
am afraid I was rather bad at playing this game. But
the point is, I think, well illustrated, that the lodgers
would expect equal treatment from the landlord, and that
he, on his side, recognized this.

It would have been interesting to know how this worked
when the wife's sister's daughter lived in the house the
year before. It might have indicated that even close kin
could not be given differential treatment, but I think
it more likely, from my observation of other cases, that
the difference between kin and non-kin would be recognized
by the lodgers. After all, I was not a member of the
family, and this gave me the borderline position
described.

Using other observations, then, I think it convenient
to distinguish between the lodger and the junior relative
in their relationship to the houseowner.

The basis of the houseowner-lodger relationship is
primarily economic: the lodger receives accommodation in
return for rent. But at the same time, this relationship
involves rank. As he is a person able to offer accommodation, the houseowner gains the prestige, whereas the fact
that the lodger lives in someone else's house relatively
reduces his. In the relationship itself, it means that
'dependence' is involved. The lodger, then, is interested
in maintaining a pure 'business' relationship in order to
emphasize his independence. The houseowner, on the other
hand, in search for 'dependants', tries to make a show of
a more familial relationship than is really the case. The
family did now and then invite the lodgers for a snack,
but the lodgers always refused it.

The junior relative, on the other hand, is not in a
position to refuse in such cases. He gets advantages not
available to the lodger, but he is very definitely a
dependant. He may also be called upon to do things the
houseowner could not ask lodgers to do. Thus I often
went to the off-licence for my landlord to buy tobacco
or whisky. In Tusharbhai's household there was a young
girl, a village-fellow of the houseowner's wife. She was
living in London because she worked there in an office -
but it was a special appointment, and her father, living
in the Midlands, would not allow her to live on her own
in London. She thus worked full time, but also ran the
house for the family and did the cooking. At the same
time she paid rent. In this case, then, being in the
position of 'junior relative' was not very advantageous
for her. On the other hand, had she not been allowed to
stay with this family, she might not have been able to
hold her job. Besides, she had a very good friend in the
house, a lodger who was a non-Patidar. This relationship
might have been difficult to sustain if she had had to
live somewhere else.

This shows that the 'dependence' is more than formal.
It may well entail services which makes it a real
advantage for the houseowner to have junior relatives in
the house. For the relatives there may be little choice,
because their parents will generally want them to stay
with people they know well. This is a factor of some
importance in the case of boys, but for girls it is often
their only possibility for living away from home unless
they break off all relations with parents, kin and
community.

As I have shown, the junior relatives and the lodgers

may well develop conflicting interests, and the borderline
between them may be difficult to draw. In a sense they
are competing for resources, since they both have transactions with the same houseowner and these are not very
different. If the 'junior relative' is very clearly
defined as such and the lodgers keep themselves to themselves, the relationship may be without much conflict.
But if the junior relatives want more independence without
foregoing their advantages, if the lodgers want more
service without becoming dependents, and the houseowner
wants more dependence from everybody, using the junior
relatives as the example for the others but at the same
time wishing to maintain some difference, the situation
may become chaotic.

The 'internal' shopkeeper

R.H. Desai treats at length the relationship between the
'internal' shopkeeper and his customers (1963, pp.58-60).
His contention is that its particular form is derived
from the contrasting influences of the jajmani system
brought over from India, and the purely commercial
relationship between customer and shopkeeper. This is
borne out by the role-play observed when the shopkeeper
visits his customers to deliver the weekly supply of
goods. He is then treated, according to Desai, as a
kamin, i.e. as a traditional servant of the jajman or
overlord. Certainly, in this relationship as manifested
during the delivery of goods, the shopkeeper is the
underling. My landlord kept up this social distance in
the way he treated 'his' grocer, looking down his nose
at him and trying to shut him up, telling me, as a
bystander, that 'this man talks too much'. But I did
not find in London, and so cannot describe, the visiting
relationship between grocer and customer that Desai
describes, whereby the grocer on his round is invited in
for tea and a chat.
    Still, I would like to add a note on his derivation of
this role-play from the jajmani system. I do not disagree,
as it seems to tally well with what I have observed in
other relationships and called either 'dependence' or
'rank'. It seems a fundamental trait of the London
Patidar community that the members interact always within
an inegalitarian framework. The role-play Desai observed
when the 'internal' shopkeeper visited his customers may
therefore be seen as just another manifestation of this
general feature of social life within the community.
    It was clear that, as in Desai's time, the 'internal'

shopkeeper had his fixed clientele among caste and village-
fellows, and that such a clientele was important for some
London shopkeepers too. But I would not make it a
condition for regarding their business as 'internal':
some of them seemed to draw their clientele from Gujaratis
or even Indians in general. But these were always
'immigrants' in Desai's sense (1963, pp.12-13), and thus
were different from the customers of the 'external'
shopkeeper.

Still, village and kin ties obviously had some
importance. But I felt this was more clearly evident in
Coventry than in London, and the explanation is probably
simply the spread of kin networks all over London as
contrasted with the relatively compact 'Indian' settlement
in Coventry. Thus in London there were not always related
shopkeepers at a practical distance from the customer, and
the competition from non-kin but Indian business made
itself felt. My landlord's wife, for example, did a
considerable part of her shopping in a Punjabi shop and
in another owned by a Catholic from Kerala, both within
walking distance.

Competition from non-Indian business also became more
significant in these circumstances. For non-Indian goods,
the supermarkets were generally able to offer lower
prices. And the factor of cost was, as I have noted in
my introductory chapter, of paramount importance. Thus
there were some Gujarati shops in the neighbourhood,
though none was run by Patidars; they were known to
Veenabai, but she denounced them as too expensive.

I am suggesting, therefore, that the different
ecological circumstances in London make the kind of
'internal' business that Desai observed in the Midlands
and the north of little importance for the London Patidars.
But this does not mean that 'internal' shopkeepers do not
exist: they just find their customers among a wider group.
Although they are not heavily restricted to the Patidar
community, but also do business with other groups of
immigrants from the subcontinent, they do not do much
business with members of the encompassing society.

The 'internal' shopkeeper is able to vary his prices
more markedly between different customers, at least when
he is delivering by van. And since members of the
encompassing society seldom enter his shop, he is able to
overcharge them, relatively speaking. Another difference
in this respect is that the internal customer will
transact much of his business in Gujarati, which again
makes differential pricing easier, not only with regard
to English customers but also Punjabis and others. The
external customer, conversely, usually tries to keep the

conversation exclusively in English even when spoken to
in Gujarati; presumably he expects that English customers
will feel 'outside' if Gujarati is spoken.

The 'internal' shopkeeper's business does not auto-
matically bring prestige. If he visits his customers, he
is even treated somewhat like a servant. The money earned
from the business, does, of course, enhance his rank, both
when he is able to persuade others that he is a good
businessman and a good saver, and when he is able to re-
invest. A 'good' shop brings prestige: but as this means
one generally catering for better-class customers, it is
a prestige usually reserved for the shops that I have
described as 'external'.

Shopkeeping seems to present a career pattern which
is exemplified in Tusharbhai's case, to be described in
the next chapter. The rungs of the ladder rise from a
humble start in one's own rooms (without a 'shop' in the
strict sense) to expansion to a shop of the 'internal'
kind: proceeds from this may be re-invested in the more
prestigious 'external' shop, and finally the really
successful man may become a wholesaler. This, of course,
means that the ranking of the steps of the ladder closely
corresponds with the amount of capital necessary for these
different kinds of business.

The bottom step of this ladder, the selling of groceries
on the side, appears to have become obsolete even in the
provinces. Though it seems to have loomed large in
Desai's time (1963, pp.60-2), I did not come across any
contemporary case.

While the shopkeeping as such may not be particularly
prestigious, it is still business, and so enjoys the
prestige generally attributed to business within the
community. It shows 'businessmanship'. The negative
prestige implications involved in visiting do not extend
to shopkeeping in general. But this negative attitude to
door-to-door sales is borne out by another case. Anilbhai
and Rameshbhai were simultaneously thinking of becoming
insurance salesmen. But Anilbhai did not like 'going
about knocking on people's doors' and so did not take that
opportunity up. Rameshbhai, however, accepted it, and
soon rose to an administrative position. The stigma lay
clearly in the 'visiting'.

To sum up, the relationship between the 'internal'
businessman and his customers is internal to the encompassed community and, in London, with it also to some
other Indian communities in a similar position. Where
there is a concentration of kin and village-fellows, as
well as caste-fellows, the 'internal' business is based
on the links provided by this fact. In London, this is

not as important as the specialization in Indian
'immigrant' goods. The fact that there are so many
Indian shops in an area, while Patidar shops may be far
away, makes kin-based business less practicable in London.
Since the home-based shop seems to have lost its significance, most shops now have a front and thus advertise
themselves to everybody.

But in spite of these factors, the 'internal' shopkeeper remains distinct from the 'external' one in that
his goods and prices are geared to suit the members of
the encompassed society rather than the British middle
class. His style is different.

The 'internal' shopkeeper is important not only for
the goods he sells. As he also keeps the latest information about Indian film-shows and social occasions,
'functions', etc., he serves as a source of information.
His position is ideal for brokerage, which I shall go
into later.

The relation between borrower and moneylender

Let me treat this relationship by relating a rather
special case, which involves Harishbhai and Ashok Patel.
Harishbhai is a worker trying to establish himself as a
broker; Ashok Patel is a young skilled worker, newly
married.

Ashok Patel's need for a loan arose when, after years
of trying, he managed to get a permit for his old mother
to come from East Africa and settle with him and his wife.
The problem was that they lived in one room in South
London and had no room for her. The wife's dowry, about
£1,000, was still in Africa with her brother, and they
could not get it out. Ashok Patel had a good steady job,
as had his wife, but no capital.

When he heard about this, Harishbhai met Ashok Patel
and suggested that he should go to Coventry, where houses
were much cheaper than in London. Harishbhai would help
him to find a house and lend him some money towards the
down payment. But this was on one condition: if Ashok
Patel were unable to pay his instalments, the house would
be taken over by Harishbhai.

Later, when Ashok Patel had made quite a few trips to
Coventry to look for a house, and after he had settled
on a certain house and had been in touch with a solicitor,
it turned out that Harishbhai had in fact no money to
lend, as he was hard up himself. He wanted to buy a house
in London and could not get a mortgage for the kind he
wanted. The loan therefore fell through with much ill
feeling on both sides.

Shortly afterwards, I related this story to Anilbhai.
He remarked immediately, about Ashok Patel: 'He's been a
fool. He should have come to me. I could have given him
the loan. I do not have the money but Rameshbhai has,
and so I could get Ashok Patel a loan with him.' He told
me to go and tell Ashok Patel. I did, but he had given
up the idea of buying a house, much embittered. Shortly
afterwards he went to some of his relatives in the north,
probably hoping to find some alternative solution to the
problem.

The most salient fact in this story is, I think, that
it is the moneylender who goes hunting for a borrower.
This is no accident; on the contrary, it is important to
see moneylending not as something indulged in mainly for
material gains but for prestige, and in order to recruit
dependants. When we were house-hunting in Coventry,
Ashok Patel, Harishbhai and I, Harisbhai was obviously
in charge all the time. He played the boss who had taken
the young man under his wing. He would say conspicuously
to outsiders: 'I am lending him the money.' We had no
choice but to accept his leadership. Once, when Harishbhai
was busy talking to the owner of a house, Ashok Patel
remarked to me (referring to Harishbhai): 'You know, this
man makes me completely sick.'

Moneylending, then, is used to foster dependence. It
is legitimate to demonstrate this by showing people the
dependant and informing them of the fact, as Anilbhai
would often do with me. But Harishbhai was overstepping
the limits of decency in this behaviour, in Ashok Patel's
view. Moneylending is, of course, sometimes business as
well. But generally its significance is not as a way in
which money is made as much as a method of telling people
that you already have it.

The broker and his clients

What I have just been saying about the moneylender applies
also to the broker. In a sense, brokering is present in
a number of other statuses, and the term may not be
thought relevant. I have chosen it, however, because it
seems the best to fit the kinds of transactions into
which the incumbent of this status enters. It obviously
is a kind of brokerage in the sense Mayer or Bailey use
the word, but I should emphasize that here it denotes but
one of the statuses described (Mayer, 1967, p.168 and
passim; Bailey, 1969). It will have been realized that
some moneylenders (looked at in one relation) may turn
out to be brokers - middlemen - for loans; this was the

role that Anilbhai was trying to play.

The basis of the broker-client relationship is the same type of transaction as that between the moneylender and his borrower: a favour of some kind is shown, and dependence – or at least a show of dependence – is obtained by the broker. The favours may be very varied: those I happened to observe included obtaining goods at a discount (or particularly tax-free or duty-free), or securing, through the personal character of the relationship, that the client is not fooled by others. (He, of course, may still be, but may perhaps not find out.) Charter-flight tickets for India or East Africa, duty-free transistors, tape recorders or television sets, used cars, stolen T-shirts and other articles of clothing (not stolen by the broker but obtained by him cheaply and with the knowledge of their origin) – almost anything can be the object of such brokerage.

Let me state again that rank and dependants are the values sought by the broker. It is important for his prestige that the ability of the broker to obtain these favours should be known in the community. As for dependence, there is clearly a considerable difference between being able to say: 'I'm lending this man the money to buy a house' and 'I got this man some cheap T-shirts.' In the last case dependence cannot be said to be involved, even for show, but in the first case it is. Charter-flights and radios are clearly somewhere in between.

Generally it can be said, however, that dependence is not involved here in any very real sense. Living in somebody's house is more important. After all, people can always buy their transistors elsewhere. But the ability to get people favours in the form of cheap goods ties in nicely with the emphasis on businessmanship, and brings respect. And for the same reason, the client is regarded as rather foolish if he does not jump on to such a good deal. If you're able to arrange or make good deals then you are somebody within the community.

Brokerage is wholly internal to the encompassed community. It does sometimes constitute a link between the broker and the people who supply the goods, which may be said to be a link to the encompassing society. But these links are insignificant as compared to the many that lead to patrons within the encompassed community ('patron' here being distinguished from 'broker' as Mayer does; 1967, p.168). In all cases, it is within the encompassed community that brokering is made known, and prestige obtained from it. The opportunity for it depends partly on the members of that community not knowing the rules of the game going on outside it.

The leaders and their public

My use of the word 'leader' here is specific. It does
not refer to leadership in a general, political sense.
As will probably be clear, many other statuses involve
'leadership' in one sense. On the other hand, there is
no formal political organization of the community, so
there are no leaders in that, also commonly accepted,
sense. People do talk of leaders, however, within the
community; what they mean are office-holders and
especially the leading office-holder of certain kinds of
organization - mainly the 'cultural organizations'. Their
main activity is to organize rituals and the festivities
connected with them, but they are not necessarily temples.
Such festive occasions, based either on traditional
religious ritual or, in some cases, on such modern
political celebrations as 'Independence Day' or 'Republic
Day', are what is universally called 'functions' by Indians
in Britain, including the London Patidars.
     Such organizations are, according to Desai, a very
recent development. He mentions a couple of associations,
but these do not have the form so common at present (1963,
pp.88-107). Particularly, he denies the existence at the
time of temples in any form, stating that 'the elaborate
rituals which are required in a temple are forbidden by
custom on foreign soil' (p.93). Since then, however,
temples have flourished and a fair number of new ones were
started while I was in England. Perhaps the East African
influx since 1960 changed the situation so completely.
Certainly, temples have existed in East Africa for a long
while, and most of the East African Indians arrived after
Desai's time. In Coventry, the 'Africans' (i.e. the East
African Indians) claimed that the temple and the Hindu
Samaj (association) was almost exclusively their own
work.   This was stated at a large meeting when the
temple was full, and it was well received by the audience.
Very likely, most of the temple-goers were themselves
'Africans', though I know that there were some 'Indians'
(i.e. those who had come straight from India) among them.
Let me add that this distinction did not seem at all
important to the Patidars (who were not present in
Coventry).
     The 'leader' is responsible for organizing these
functions, and much work goes into this. In London
particularly, where there was an element of competition
between different leaders and their associations, great
care was taken to make the function as sumptuous as
possible. This was not confined to the function itself:
programmes were printed which were expensively ornate

and very elegant indeed. I have two such programmes that are particularly impressive: these were issued by Sarobhai Patel's association.

The organization of functions, then, brings the organizer great prestige. It seems always to be upon him rather than the association that this prestige is bestowed; others, who may have partly financed the occasion, receive theirs mostly by their advertisements in the programme. This, besides, gives the names of the committee, and being on a committee is in itself prestigious.

The audience, or public at a function acknowledge the prestige and high rank of the organizer. Often he himself is on the stage as master of ceremonies, introducing the function and the items on the programme. He is seen by everybody, and is seen to be important.

What the public receives in return is quite simply the fun. A good function is something to be seen, with its combination of religious, folk and purely artistic elements. Sometimes the whole thing is a real work of art; this was true, for example, of the two functions I saw that Tusharbhai and his song-and-dance group had staged. He, incidentally, was also the producer of a play in English which was well received.

Apart from the functions, associations of this kind do not play a significant political role. This role is largely left to the 'top leader', to whom I shall return. His view of the associations and their leaders, however, is of relevance here: he thought they had very little real influence and were mainly good for their cultural role. There are different associations with a slightly different base, however, and I shall discuss them in chapter 7.

Another type of association, which does have real influence, is that of different kinds of Indian craftsmen. I spoke to the then Chairman of the Indian Goldsmiths' Association who lived in Smethwick. But since they are not craftsmen, not many Patidars can join them.

In Africa, the Patidars had several specific caste organizations (Morris, 1968, p.100) but I did not find any in London.

Another enterprise which clearly belongs here is the Gujarati newspaper - a fortnightly - and its editor. The paper claims to have a circulation of 4,000 (some informants thought that this must be an overstatement) and is read by a number of the leading personalities of the community. The editor is at the same time the London correspondent for a number of Gujarati papers.

The leaders, generally, do not receive any material

advantage from their functions. They may, on the other
hand, risk a considerable amount of money as well as
waste a good deal of work if it is not successful. It is
done purely for prestige. It is probably well also to
include some idealism as a motive: some have an idea of
organizing the Indians in England to protect their
interests, and good 'functions' may possibly lead to
communication with the English middle class. The first
motive does not seem to have brough about much in the
way of organization, but as a communication of cultural
identity to the British the functions may have played
some part. Certainly the rituals and their implication
of maintaining Indian identify and self-respect in the
foreign setting are important for the members of the
community itself.

THE TERTIARY STATUSES

I have not described the 'external' shopkeeper's transactions with the incumbents of secondary statuses because
a number of the presentations involved are not sought by
him. He can therefore avoid the dependence that is
involved in entering into some of these transactions from
below, as it were. Normally, he himself owns a house.
He is himself in an excellent position to act as a
broker. He does not seek the services that the 'internal'
shopkeeper has to offer. As a businessman, he is in a
different position with regard to the encompassing
society from the worker. He, in all probability, knows
more about 'the rules of the game' outside his own
community.

In short, instead of entering into the position of the
worker as shown in Figure 3, he chooses to convert his
returns from the business into one or more of the
secondary statuses. This may result in an increase in
general prestige, in the number of dependants or in
monetary profits.

Such a possibility is open also to the 'internal'
shopkeeper. But even the worker can invest by entering
one of the five statuses mentioned. From the returns of
his work he may achieve a position where he is able to lend
small sums or buy a house. He may set up shop as an
'internal' shopkeeper, as seems to have been even more
common earlier. Through contacts with people offering a
variety of services, he may become a broker. Finally, if
he is well liked and has the contacts, he might enter the
committee of one of the leaders.

How this is all done is the subject of the next

chapter. But I have already mentioned a third level of
statuses: these I shall call 'wholesaler', 'agent' and
'top leader'.

I have relatively few data on these people; some of
them are outside the encompassed Patidar community proper,
and belong rather to that small stratum of upper-class
Indian businessmen in London which are outside the scope
of my study. However, since these statuses are attainable
by members of the encompassing society, and since some,
such as the top leader, are members of it, I shall include
them here.

A further reason is that much that goes on at lower
levels can be understood only when these tertiary statuses
are taken into account.

The wholesaler, then, relates both to 'external' and
'internal' shopkeepers who both exchange goods for cash.
At the same time, the wholesaler's status ranks higher in
the view of the community members, but this reflects
general businessmanship and is not a result of specific
expressions of dependence on the shopkeeper's side. In a
purely economic sense, however, he clearly is very much
dependent on the Indian wholesaler specializing in Indian
goods, without whom he would have to import them himself.

The agent may have an import-export business, or he
may provide cheap charter-flights. Generally in connection
with import-export, he may be able to provide radios,
television sets, tape-recorders, etc., duty-free or tax-
free. He usually operates through brokers, though he may
also sell direct. The broker may receive cash as
commission, but on the whole it is not primarily an
economic activity for him. It is with the agent that most
of the material gain remains.

The top leader has a status held by one incumbent only.
He is the only member of the encompassed community in a
position of influence with British officialdom. Thus he
is much in demand for help and advice in obtaining entry
permits, labour vouchers, etc. He is able to pursue these
matters efficiently, notably in his capacity as secretary
of the Committee on Commonwealth Citizenship. In this
capacity he serves not only the Patidars, but other
Indians, and indeed other Commonwealth immigrants, as well.

The top leader is thus able to obtain by means of his
relationship with officials services highly valued by the
members of the encompassed community. From the point of
view of the British, I can only assume that the reason for
maintaining this connection is the need to communicate
with someone of influence within the immigrant groups.
The fact that the top leader also heads the important
Patidar community with a large number of people must surely
be relevant.

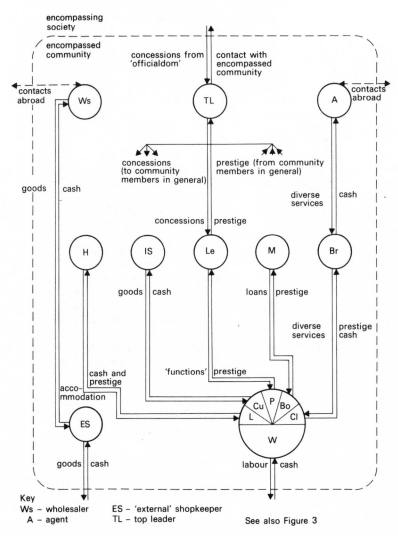

FIGURE 4   Transactional structure

Within the encompassed community, other minor leaders often act as intermediaries for communication with the top leader. This kind of 'brokering' is most useful for them vis à vis the rank and file. They are thus able to legitimise their position as leaders. For the top leader, however, this indirect communication is not always the most suitable, and he seems to prefer direct contact whenever possible.

Because of his position, the top leader may be accused of accepting bribes to obtain services. I have never been able to substantiate this claim, but the same could be true of the claimants themselves. I myself do not believe he does: my general impression of the top leader as a person was that of a very astute but essentially honest politician whose efficiency was above question.

The pattern of transactions between all three statuses are set out in Figure 4, which represents what might be called the structure, or at least the economic structure, of the encompassed Patidar community. I shall avoid that term, however, for the connotation of permanence it seems to imply. Figure 3 depicts no more than some of the statuses relevant to economic life within the community; the pattern of interactions between them thus defines the statuses. Such a diagram dannot indicate any idea of change: it describes the London Patidar community in 1969-70. It was not, as I have tried to make clear, like this in 1957-61 when Desai did his fieldwork, and will probably be different again in some years' time.

6 Strategies and value conversions

The pattern of transactions I have outlined above gives
an idea of the statuses, as the positions from which
transactions are made, and of the types of transactions
going on between their incumbents. But these are only
elements of what Barth terms 'form' (see chapter 1 and
Barth, 1966, Introduction). First, these statuses may
be said to constitute stepping-stones in the strategies
and the resultant career of any one individual in the
community. Second, form is really the sum total of the
cumulative results of these strategies at any specified
time. Thus, in order to describe form, it is necessary
not only to set out the types of statuses, transactions
and strategies, but also to give some more or less exact
idea of the numerical distribution of these types within
the community.

I shall describe the strategies of London Patidars by
relating a few cases, which I shall analyse as far as
possible within the terms of reference provided by the
statuses and relationships already mentioned.

CASE NO.1

Some account of Anilbhai was given in chapter 4, and his
case will now be examined in more detail. The job he
found on arrival in a northern city was car painting. He
thus became a worker, and, while in the north, lived with
other Indians as a lodger. He was helped in finding
accommodation by other immigrants from his home town. In
1961 he moved to London, where he had a different job
with the same firm. Here he was given a room in the house
of another village-mate (N.A. Desai) in north London. He
is still in touch with this landlord, and the rank
difference between them is still clear. This man is a

Brahmin, which may partly account for their relative rank.

In 1964 he brought his wife over from India, and in
1965 his two sons. (He had visited India at intervals.)
In 1966 his father came to see them. They were then still
in rented accommodation, though they had moved away from
the Brahmin and were at one time living in a Greek house.
The father, they told me, 'did not like the way they were
living' and so Anilbhai was given a loan by his father
(who had been a businessman in Fiji before retiring to
India) towards the down payment for a house. He himself
had also been saving, and so was able to provide the
larger part of the payment himself. The house he chose
was a big one in inner north London, for which he seems
to have had no difficulty in getting a mortgage for a
term of twenty years.

Once he had bought the house, he retained two rooms
for his own use and let the other five (more than his
mortgage arrangements allowed him to let). The rooms
were rented with half board; i.e. two meals a day except
Sundays. His wife, who till then had been working in a
factory, stayed at home to cook for the lodgers.

He had now well and truly become a houseowner and was
using this status to make money. As mentioned above, he
was also interested in making the lodgers his 'dependants',
but he cannot be said to have completely succeeded in
this. In the balance between making money or making
dependants out of houseowning, he seems to have put the
stress on the former.

His work in the car paintshop gave him some opportunity
for making money on the side. Sometimes he fixed up an
old car, using the workshop premises, and sold it. Sometimes he could obtain cheap goods (mostly clothing, etc.)
through contacts at work and re-sold them within the
community. Through contacts with other people from his
home town, particularly Rameshbhai who was a relative and
Tusharbhai, who came from his wife's village, he was able
to exploit the broker status. He put customers in touch
with Tusharbhai for such things as cheap charter flights,
but he took no commission. Through Rameshbhai he obtained
loans for his clients, to whom he thus became a moneylender
as well.

In Figure 5 I have tried to illustrate Mr Patel's use
of the available statuses. We can see that he is now
acting as a middleman in more than one respect, and in
addition is the direct source of accommodation for a
number of workers and students. Through his transactions
he acquires money, and also prestige and some dependants.
But he also has to acknowledge the higher rank of people
such as Tusharbhai and Rameshbhai in order to maintain his
transactions as a broker.

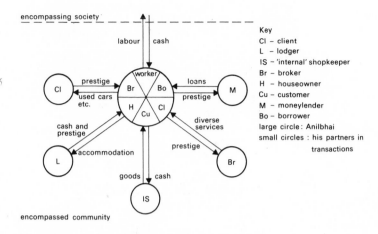

FIGURE 5   Anilbhai's use of statuses

Figure 6 depicts the value conversions made by Mr Patel. Work for wages produces cash, which has been invested in the house (including the mortgage payments). The house is run as a business with the help of the wife's labour as an input. This business again brings in cash, and also establishes him as a houseowner, thus giving him rank. Some cash as well as some spare-time work is invested in old cars, etc.; this gives him a cash profit on their re-sale. Further spare-time work is invested in other kinds of brokering, which enhance his rank. All these investments are cumulative in effect, since rank gained as a broker gives him access to new clients. Finally, his savings may be re-invested in the house, and this he plans to do in one of two ways. Either, he says, he will invest some more money in the old house: he would then like to convert the upper part into self-contained flats. This would keep rent income at the same or near the present level, and then the wife would be free to go out to work, earning more money. The other alternative is to buy a small house for himself in south London, closer to his work now that his firm has moved, and let the whole north London house. This, again, would free the wife to earn money outside, and would keep the income from rent at a satisfactory level.

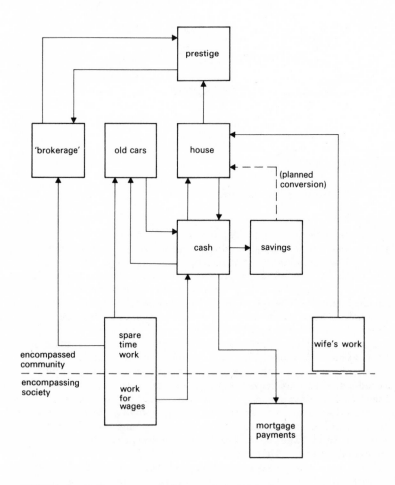

FIGURE 6   Value conversions of Anilbhai

CASE NO.2

Tusharbhai arrived in England at the age of twenty-two
from East Africa, and went into business as an 'internal'
shopkeeper in Birmingham, where he eventually owned five
small shops. He had thus gained enough capital to set

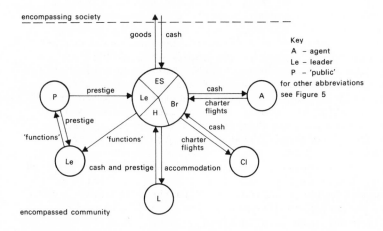

FIGURE 7   Tusharbhai's use of statuses

himself up in London as an 'external' shopkeeper. His
shop is among the best of its kind in London; as well as
being a kind of delicatessen, it also specializes in
health foods. In association with other Indians, he has
embarked upon other kinds of business also, such as
catering. He has also acted as the main broker for an
agent for cheap charter-flights whose office is above is
shop. An older caste-mate is employed to produce Indian
savouries and sweets, also working over the shop. With
an English businessman, he intends to enter wholesale
business in the health food trade. He is in many ways
quite a remarkable personality, as he is not preoccupied
with business and money but invests a great deal of time
and money in cultural activity. He has formed a music-
and-dance company which performs at functions, and also
produced a play in English written by another well-known
Indian in London. He writes poetry, is an extremely
strict vegetarian, a strict teetotaller, and holds
'traditional' attitudes to sex and to the Indian life
style in general. He has a large flat and takes in
lodgers.

I have tried to depict in Figure 7 the positions he
occupies in terms of the transactional structure.

His main livelihood is of course earned through selling
goods in his shop. As he is an 'external' shopkeeper, he
has very many dealings with members of the encompassing
society. To some extent this in itself gives him high
rank within the encompassed community, because his shop
is of such a high quality (I shall return to this). As

an 'external' shopkeeper he does not have any typical
transactions with other members of the encompassed
community.

In his position as a 'broker', however, such transactions are very much in evidence. Through this status
he, like Anilbhai, obtains rank. But it does also bring
him cash, since he has had a fixed arrangement with the
charter-flight agent. But I think that it is the rank
that is still important. He can assure customers about
information on such flights as well as provide some
measure of personal guarantee that the flights are
reliable.

Strictly speaking, he is not a houseowner, but he does
have lodgers in his large flat right in the centre of
London. In his relationships with these lodgers, I can
find no reason to distinguish him from people who own a
whole house. He thus receives both cash and rank in
return for the accommodation he is able to offer.

His position as a leader is slightly special, since
he is to a large extent offering other leaders the main
items for entertainment at their functions and still
does not stand - in the eyes of those attending them -
as the man responsible for them. Thus he does not
receive the respect pertaining to that position. The
leader, however, will usually thank him publicly, saying
that without him the function would not have been
possible - which is quite true - and so some of the rank
earned by the man responsible for it ultimately devolves
upon Tusharbhai. The other leaders are aware of his
abilities, moreover, and his part in the arrangement and
so accept him as a leader like themselves.

But it should also be said that Tusharbhai obviously
does not regard himself primarily as an 'immigrant
leader' but as an intellectual, as understood by the
encompassing society's members. Such an idiom is shared
with the members of the westernized cultural elite in
India. It is perhaps not irrelevant, on this point,
that he himself lived in Bombay as well as in East Africa.

On the whole, Figure 7 shows the strategies of
Tusharbhai to be oriented towards rank and 'culture'
rather than towards increasing his money income.

From the flow chart (Figure 8) which is intended to
show the conversion of values which his strategies imply,
the same conclusion can be drawn. Tusharbhai in his shop
converts labour and a cash investment into goods, which
he sells in the shop - he thereby also adds the investment
of his wife's labour, which he controls. This gives a
cash return. Some of it is invested in the house and
some in the music-and-dance society, i.e. in functions.

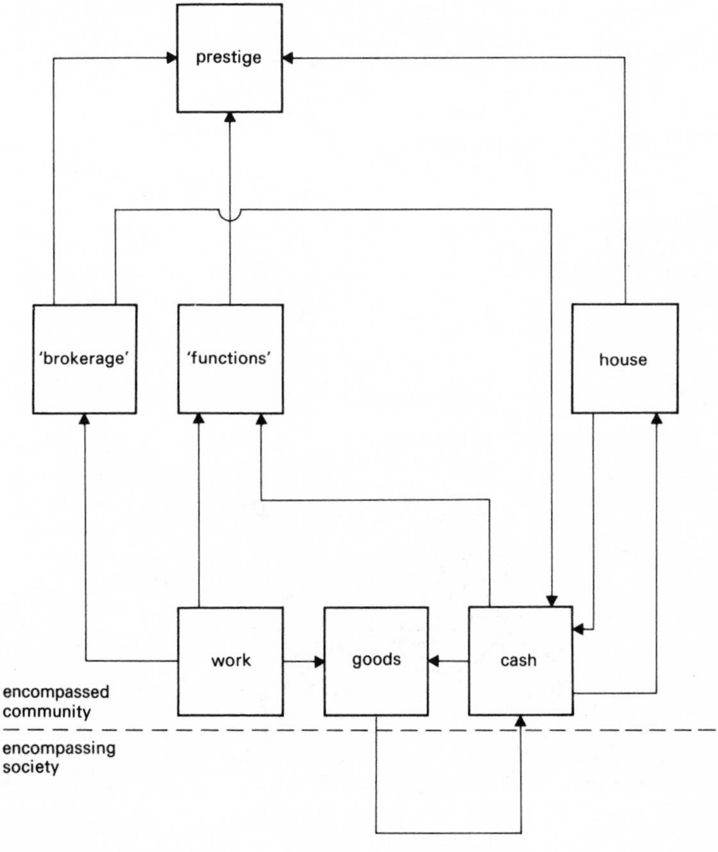

FIGURE 8 Value conversions of Tusharbhai

In the first instance there is both a cash and a rank
return. Incidentally, the offer of accommodation also
enabled him to employ a young girl to cook for the
members of the household. She, like the other lodgers,
also paid rent to Tusharbhai. In the second instance,
the investment of cash and labour in the song-and-dance
group gives him rank. Finally, some labour is converted
into brokering, and thereby into rank.

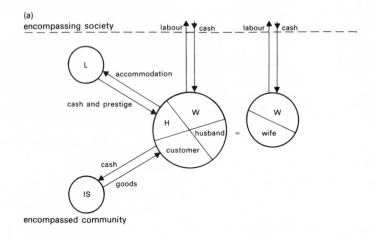

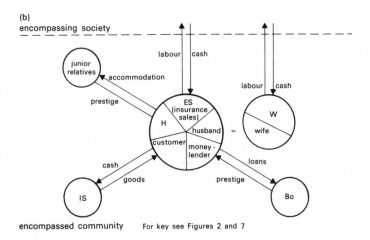

FIGURE 9   Rameshbhai's use of statuses

CASE NO.3

The third case, Rameshbhai, was a driving instructor
running his own business in Nairobi who on arrival in
England took up the same kind of business, establishing
himself in south London. But he was not very successful,
and after some time decided to close down. The capital
he gained from the sale of his business he invested in
two houses in a northern city. He then became a houseowner who rented out a house and a half. At the same time

he took a job as a bus driver. His wife, a qualified
nurse, had no difficulty finding suitable work.

It is appropriate first to describe his position in
terms of the transactional statuses he occupied at this
stage before I go on to recount his later career. This
position is set out in Figure 9(a).

This figure shows few new features. In this situation,
Rameshbhai has not gained much rank. What there is
results mainly from his houseownership, but he does
receive cash from three sources: his work, the rent, and
his wife's work.

His total annual income at this stage he estimated to
be £4,000.

This cash was obviously intended to produce capital
for future business investments. While he was in the
situation I have described, however, something else
happened. A foreign investment company was setting up
its sales force in Britain. It based this enterprise
upon the 'Dover plan', a combination of an investment
plan and life insurance. As I indicated in chapter 5,
Anilbhai and Rameshbhai were interested in this kind of
work, but Anilbhai rejected it as being too embarrassing:
he did not like to go about knocking on people's doors,
whereas Rameshbhai took the job. As an insurance
salesman, he did very well indeed, and starting from
part-time, was ultimately promoted to be a branch manager,
an executive position which entailed moving back to
London. House prices being rather higher there, however,
he had to sell one of his houses in the north. When the
family moved to London, his wife took up work again as a
nurse. Their house was now a family house, though one
young female relative stayed with them. I do not know
the family's total earnings in London, but I have reason
to believe that they were considerably higher than in the
north - probably in the region of £5,000.

In London, Rameshbhai also took on the status of
moneylender. Curiously, however, he did not let his
remaining house in the north but used it occasionally
when he travelled there on business.

In Figure 9(b), I have tried to set out his position
in London. The pattern of value conversions demarcates
three srages in his career. Figure 10 shows each of
these stages as well as the connections between them.

In the north, cash was very clearly the main motive
(stage 2). In London, however, a further increase in
rank ensued.

His rank in London (stage 3) was obtained partly by
exploiting the moneylender status, but Rameshbai indulged
in some conspicuous consumption as well: he bought a

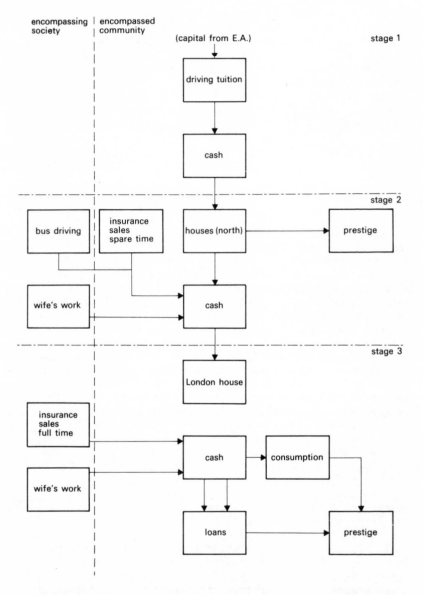

FIGURE 10   Value conversions of Rameshbhai

Plymouth Barracuda V8 automatic – a very efficient status symbol. Anilbhai's boys and I were certainly not the only people affected by the car's appeal.

This position, then, gives him rank through moneylending

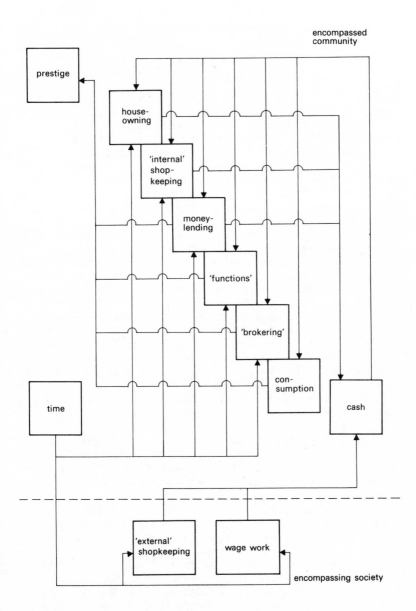

FIGURE 11 Summary of strategies

and conspicuous consumption. He is independent of brokers,
for he is himself well informed and has contacts.

CONCLUSION: STRATEGIES OPEN TO THE ACTORS

In Figure 11 I have tried to summarize the strategies
open to the actors in terms of value conversions and re-
investment. The three cases described above give some
idea of how the London Patidars use the statuses described
in chapter 5 to get ahead. Some do not get very far, and
do not exploit any status other than that of worker.
These may be the majority. But people like Anilbhai,
Tusharbhai and Rameshbhai prove to others that it is
possible to progress, and thus in a sense show the way.
They and others like them become trend-setters, in varying
degrees. When I say that they demonstrate that it is
possible to get ahead, I am not implying that this is
objectively possible for every single immigrant, as I
discuss in the conclusion. But I do imply that these, as
'success stories', prove to other immigrants that
'Indians may get along here' or 'Patidars may do quite
well here' and thus maintain an ideology of success. This
ideology, of course, rests on the basis that the immigrants
are supposed to start more or less from the same point.
It does not take into account any significant differences
in the backgrounds of individuals.

Seen in this light, such relatively successful cases
become outstandingly important. For the analysis
attempted here, it is equally valuable to attempt some
generalization as to what kinds of strategies are available
to the London Patidar who longs for success. This is what
Figure 11 attempts to do, and I shall comment briefly on
the choices - the stages - along the way.

I assume an immigrant has just arrived. He may or may
not have any capital to speak of; if he comes from East
Africa, he is more likely to have some funds. He sells
his work for wages or, if he has capital, may at once set
up in business. Thus he becomes an 'external' or
'internal' shopkeeper. In both cases he does get some
cash; if he is a good saver, he is soon able to re-invest
it. In most cases, also, he is in a position to choose
whether to work all day and evenings too in his job or
shop or alternatively to invest some of this time in work
in a field such as brokering or functions. Most likely,
however, he is not familiar enough with the situation to
be able to do this just yet. Stage 1, then, of his stay
is likely to be dedicated exclusively to making money
from the above sources.

In stage 2 he is likely to have some savings. This is
the time for looking round for ways of re-investing that
money profitably. The secondary statuses then become
important, and offer quite a wide choice of activities.

House-buying needs a large amount of capital, at least in London; but it is one possible means for re-investment. This would benefit his rank as well as his economic position.   In the same way, the other choices have their different advantages and drawbacks.   So at a certain point, he may have been successful in establishing himself in a couple of such statuses to supplement his initial position. He may then be said to have settled down economically, and only sometimes will he still try intensively to expand in order to exploit even more statuses.

Without need for further comment, Figure 11 shows how money may be re-invested.   Rank, too, is in a sense re-invested: prestige, perhaps as a broker, is likely to produce more clients.

Another fact does call for comment.   The figure represents the value conversion possible at this stage of the development of the community.   Clearly, all the transactions it implies and which were set out in Figure 4, had once to be initiated.   Opening up these channels of conversion was clearly a story of entrepreneurship (Barth, 1963, p.12), and I shall take up this theme briefly in the conclusion.

I think I have outlined the actual strategies of certain actors as well as an overall view of established choices.   Form, however, is the result of all these actors' strategies.   What kind of community emerges?

7 Form

The immediate questions in the discussion of form must be: How are the members of the encompassed Patidar community distributed among the statuses outlined? And, since they evidently are able to fill more than one of these statuses, what combinations occur?

It is at this point that the limitations inherent in my fieldwork method become most obvious. The hundred or so people I actually can number as informants are not a very large part of the Patidars in London. I do try in Table 2 to give some tabulated answers to these questions. Twenty-five adult men are included: an unimpressive number, but the table and the notes do speak for themselves. That it is easy to combine statuses is, I think, borne out. Moreover, the most influential people tend to occupy a relatively large number of statuses: thus Sarobhai Patel, one of the leaders, occupies five. These adult men did not all live in London.

The main point of this table, then, as I see it, is that all kinds of combinations can be expected to occur in a larger sample. Further, the distribution of statuses of individuals is not clearly stratified. The stratification which may have seemed implicit in Figure 4 is not borne out when we turn to individual people.

This is obviously an important aspect of form. What it means is that there really is some possibility for social climbing within the community. It shows that even an 'ordinary worker', through one or more of the 'secondary' statuses, can climb to a rank somewhere in the middle of the community's range. Such exploitation of a 'secondary' status would show others that the man in question had 'businessmanship', and he would benefit by being highly regarded. The merchant ideology, then, gives everyone - or almost everyone - some chance of a reasonably high rank within the community, and this is obviously important for the maintenance of such an ideology.

TABLE 2

Person	Stu-dent	W	ES	IS	M	H	LE	BR	A	WS	TL
		X									
Anilbhai		X			X	X		X			
I.P.Patel			X			X					
M.L.Patel		X									
N.P.Desai		X				X (4)					
Tusharbhai			X			X	X	X		X	
N.T.Patel		X				X (1)	X				
	X										
		X									
Rameshbhai			X (6)	X (6)	X	X (1) (5)					
N.T's relative	X										
Jayant Patel		X									
The astrologer			X (3)	X (3)		X (4)					
P.J.Patel			X			X					
Harishbhai		X			X	X (1)		X			
The Bania						X			X		
S.S.Patel		X									
Top Leader			X								X
Sarobhai Patel			X (2)	X (2)		X (1)	X	X			
Ashok Patel		X									
		X				X (1)					
		X				X (1)					
		X				X (2)					
Kumar		X									
Tusharbhai's employee		X									
Total 25	2	15	7	3	3	14	3	4	1	1	1

(1) Houses where all inhabitants are related.
(2) A solicitor.
(3) An astrologer.
(4) Owns 4 houses.
(5) Owns 2 houses.
(6) Insurance agent on a managerial level. He resembles
    the internal shopkeeper when he is selling the policies
    door-to-door. He is also selling to outsiders from
    the encompassing society. Most of his time is spent
    in managerial work.

I should now remark briefly upon an aspect of the
method I followed. Most monographs on social anthropology
start by giving the reader an overall picture of form.
In studying an urban minority, spread throughout many parts
of London, however, such an overall picture appears at a
very late stage in the anthropologist's experience. And
from my very small number of informants, a direct
generalization from observations of individual cases of
form to the general form of the community would not be
firmly based. However, by analysing the statuses my
informants recognize - in this case focusing upon the
economic statuses - and then analysing their strategies,
a kind of pattern emerges. Probably it would also be
possible to understand the others in respect of this
framework, since statuses are something that people in
society have to agree upon. So the description resulting
from this kind of analysis may make the significant
features easier to identify out of the very scattered
information available about the community as a whole.
The description may therefore be of some value.

The Patidar community in London is not remarkable for
any high degree of organization. What is typical is the
scattered households, each a unit clearly headed by
someone who is likely to be a houseowner. Some families,
of course, live in houses owned by outside people. In
such cases, however, the head still has much the same
position internally as a houseowner has: the relation to
junior relatives or to lodgers (in the quite usual case
of sub-letting) is the same. Sometimes two people share
a house or flat as equal partners, but this does not
seem too common: in such cases, one of them externally
assumes the position of head.

The households are widely scattered and there seems
to be, as I have mentioned, no marked tendency for kin
and co-villagers to cluster geographically; this is
different from the situation in the provinces, where such
clustering is usual.

The place of kinship, therefore, may seem to be
insignificant. This is not because kinship ties are not
utilized. On the contrary, there is a great interest in
recognizing the presence of kinsmen, close or distant, as
well as affinal relations, in London and in Britain
generally. But clearly it is not any rule or circumstance
of kinship that decides whether an individual is in
Britain - except in the case of very close kin. Thus
relatives are relatives, but a man who is a cousin in the
second degree may be treated as a much closer kinsman, if
that is practical for both parties. Barth has recently
written:

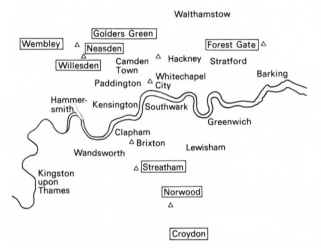

Willesden – places where 'many Patidars live'.

△ – homes of some of the people studied and mentioned
in this study (approximate).

FIGURE 12   Geographical distribution

I am arguing essentially that we should consider the
'we - they' confrontation that the social interaction
contains ... and inspect how the experience of who
'they' are will mould the actor's conception of 'we'.
This was written in a discussion of the concept of
descent, but is clearly relevant here. The point is, I
think, that in a social universe containing mostly non-
kin, particular kinship relations and their concomitant
obligations become incorporated in a general view of 'kin'
and in obligations resulting from the new situation as
well as general ideas of reciprocity.

It would clearly have been interesting, from the point
of view of kinship studies, to compare the resultant

TABLE 3   Number of telephones held by people named Patel by postal district

E		N		NW		W	
E1	2	N1	3	NW1	3	W1	5
E2	1	N2	4	NW2	48	W2	6
E3	2	N3	7	NW3	5	W3	0
E4	0	N4	9	NW4	19	W4	2
E5	1	N5	0	NW5	12	W5	1
E6	3	N6	0	NW6	24	W6	5
E7	15	N7	2	NW7	1	W7	2
E8	0	N8	4	NW8	1	W8	0
E9	0	N9	3	NW9	10	W9	0
E10	1	N10	0	NW10	40	W10	0
E11	2	N11	0	NW11	18	W11	2
E12	2	N12	5			W12	7
E13	0	N13	1			W13	2
E14	0	N14	0			W14	5
E15	3	N15	0			W15	0
E16	0	N16	0			etc. All	0
E17	0	N17	1				
E18	2	N18	0				
E19 etc.all	0	N19	6				
		N20	0				
		N21	0				
		N22	3				
		N23	0				
Total E 33		Total N 48		Total NW 181		Total W 37	

SW				WC		EC		SE			
SW1	0	SW14	0	WC1	3	EC4	1	SE1	0	SE14	0
SW2	4	SW15	1	WC2	2	etc. all	0	SE2	0	SE15	1
SW3	0	SW16	19					SE3	0	SE16	0
SW4	4	SW17	13					SE4	0	SE17	0
SW5	0	SW18	0					SE5	1	SE18	4
SW6	0	SW19	4					SE6	0	SE19	0
SW7	0	SW20	1					SE7	1	SE20	0
SW8	4	etc. All	0					SE8	0	SE21	0
SW9	5							SE9	1	SE22	0
SW10	0							SE10	1	SE23	0
SW11	2							SE11	2	SE24	2
SW12	8							SE12	1	SE25	3
SW13	0							SE13	1	SE26	1
										SE27	3
										etc. all	0
Total SW 65				Total WC 5		Total EC 1		Total SE 22			

Total telephones London 392

pattern with that existing in Charottar, but I do not
have this information.

The ecology, as it manifests itself through the cost
of housing, does influence settlement patterns.   In
Figure 12, I show some of the main settlement areas, as
assessed generally by the London Patidars.   The pattern
of settlement shows a concentration in what may be called
lower-middle-class areas, although Golders Green is an
exception, being the place where the really successful
Patidars live, according to popular belief.   Few people
have settled as far in as the older suburbs of Islington
or Camden Town; most live just a bit farther out, in
Victorian housing.

Though I could not assess the accuracy of this
distribution pattern by any complete survey, I did try
to check it in two ways, both with very obvious short-
comings.   First, I made a count of the addresses given
under the name 'Patel' in the London telephone directories.
While I am aware that such a count will include only those
who have their own telephone (and, very likely, their own
house), I am also aware that not everyone called 'Patel'
is necessarily a Patidar.   With these cautionary remarks,
however, it does seem that this count bears out the
statements above as to where Patidars in London live.
The numbers, by postal district (Table 3), show a marked
concentration in one large contiguous area stretching,
roughly, from Wembley to Golders Green.   In this area,
close to half of the telephones are concentrated.   Two
other concentrations stand out: one in SW 16 and SW 17,
i.e., the Balham-Streatham area, and E7, i.e. in Stratford
and Forest Gate.

Second, I analysed the addresses of my own Patidar
informants in the same way.   The result is given in Table
4.   Here I included only households that I visited or
knew fairly well.   It will be seen that in relation to
the other data, central as well as north London are over-
represented.   But the greatest number were still found
in NW 10, and almost as many in or near Streatham.

What is the form of these households?   It may be
convenient to distinguish between types, although these
are, however, as emerges very clearly from Desai's
description of them, often merely stages in a development
process.   It may safely be said that among Patidars (as
apparently among other immigrant groupings from the
Indian subcontinent) there has been a gradual general
movement from 'bachelor households' to 'family households'.
An excellent description of such a movement is found in
Desai (1963, pp.31-5).   Aurora describes a Sikh settlement
at the 'bachelor' stage (1967, pp.50-3), when 60 per cent

TABLE 4   Geographical distribution of informants

	Total	Adult men
N1	7	2
N7	2	1
N4	3	2
N3	3	1
NW6	4	1
NW10	10	3
WC1	1	1
WC2	6	3
W3	2	2
W11	2	1
SW4	3	2
SW16	9	3
	52	22

of the households could still be so described. When I
was in London, most Patidar households contained nuclear
families, but there were often additional members of the
household belonging to either what I have called the
'lodger' or the 'junior relative' category. The households I studied may therefore perhaps most conveniently
be divided between those where paying lodgers were and
were not present.

The first I shall describe fully is that of Mr Patel,
at the time I was living there (Figure 13). They lived
in a neo-classical terraced house built about 1880, in
a lower-middle-class road. It had six bedrooms on three
floors, a lounge in the basement, a large kitchen with
a tub built in, and a back garden. It was bought for
£7,000 in 1965.

The owner's nuclear family occupied the basement,
including the kitchen, and the sitting-room, as well as
one of the ground-floor bedrooms. I lived at first in
this room (A). In the other ground-floor bedroom lived
one of the lodgers, Sunil Modi. His brother, Shirish
Modi, had a single room on the first floor. These two
were Banias and students. A Hindu lawyer, Mr Dhruv,
lived in the second-floor single room. On the first
floor two Jain brothers, Karamchand Shah and Mohan Shah,
shared a double room, and on the second floor two
Ismaili accountancy students, Ali and Amin, shared another
double room. Thus a large part of the house was let to
non-kin, but all were Gujarati-speakers who ate Gujarati
food.

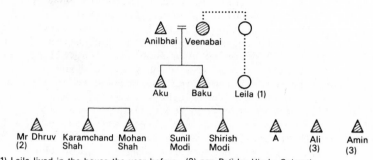

(1) Leila lived in the house the year before   (2) non-Patidar Hindu Gujarati
(3) Ismailis   A = anthropologist

FIGURE 13   Anilbhai's household

For about a year, Mrs Patel's sister's daughter, Leila,
lived in the boys' room. There was, therefore, a combination of lodgers and a junior relative in the house.

It will be clear that the inhabitants clearly divide
into the family proper and their lodgers. My own status
was ambiguous; I was living at first in the family's own
room and sleeping in a bed which, the year before, had
been used by the wife's sister's daughter. My position
was therefore at first rather that of a paying guest than
of a lodger proper.

How did the individual inhabitants come to be living
in the house?

The owner

In choosing the house, the owner says, he thought mainly
of two things: easy access to the underground, and good
schools within reach. He mentioned not only primary
schools, but also drew my attention to the closeness of
two technical colleges. He did not directly refer to the
fact that the house was a good economic proposition, but
his use of it does not leave much room for doubt that this
was very important indeed.

The wife and the children clearly are not present in
the house for independent reasons, and I shall assume that
they were there as dependants of the owner.

The graduate student

This man was a Bania who was born in 1929. His parents

lived in Bombay and from his judgment of other people's
rank it seems clear that the family must have been upper
middle class. He studied at Poona, became a lawyer, and
settled down to practise in a small village in Surat
district. Here to took to politics and journalism, fields
in which he still hopes to be a success. The village had
a very depressing effect on him; he grew thin and
despondent from the surrounding poverty and so took up an
offer to go to England for further studies, as an
opportunity to get away from the village. Here, he
stayed at a Catholic hostel for three years, having
previously been working in Leicester for a while to
finance his studies. He rented a single room in the
house for three months. He said he wanted to get away
from the hostel because, he complained: 'If everybody in
the house has a girl in his room, it is very difficult to
concentrate on work.' To find peace for his studies,
then, was why he left the hostel. He chose not to pay
for meals, taking breakfast only, an arrangement which
the owner, as he claimed, did not normally allow. From
what his astrologer told him, he said that no success in
private life was likely to come his way, but he had a
chance of becoming successful in public life and was
devoted to this aim.

The Hindu and Jain students from the Sudan

These four lodgers stayed in the house for two years -
quite a long time. The two Jain brothers shared a double
room. They took their meals in the house and were regular
in every way, like the other pair of brothers. The owner
described these four as 'his best lodgers'.
     One of the four was much concerned about his joint
family, and though he hoped to go to Canada to gain
experience, was determined about wishing to keep the
family together. At least these were his views after
seeing 'Khandan', a typical Hindi film, which depicted the
tragedy of a family divided. From similar arrangements
made by two other brothers near by, and from Gujarati
students I met elsewhere, this concern seems to be fairly
typical. This boy definitely had to take care of his
brother, who was only fifteen, but even so, I think that
the reason for brothers preferring to stay together is
not purely economic. These students saw themselves much
more as representatives of the family collectivity than
do most Western students.
     Two main factors probably led to these four staying in
the house: first, the wish to stay in an Indian and

preferably in a Gujarati house, chiefly because of the
food (all four are strict vegetarians); second - as they
all came at about the same time - they seem to have chosen
this particular house for the sake of staying together,
since the families knew each other in Sudan. They went
out together to some extent, and sometimes gathered in the
most convenient room to cook a meal of their own.

The Ismaili students

The two Ismailis from East Africa who shared the top floor
double room had stayed previously at a hostel mainly for
students in Bayswater. Becoming friends there, and
desiring more independence, they decided to move out.
They still went to the hostel fairly frequently to meet
friends. One of them said that if they had not found this
accommodation, he would probably have gone to live in the
Ismaili Cultural Centre, a mosque and hostel near Kensington High Street. They both came from business families.
In search of further independence, they were looking for
accommodation without meals. They were less dependent on
living in an Indian house partly because they were not
vegetarians. They were also more fond of Western than
Indian films, and had a liking for pubs. Their conversation was more about sex than that of the Hindu and Jain
boys, and they therefore openly mentioned the restrictions
against girls in the room - I never heard the others make
this complaint.

A day in the house

First awake and up was Mr Patel himself. To get to work
at 7, he rose at about 5. Though Gujaratis generally
rise much earlier than most English, he did sometimes
complain about it.

He prepared his own breakfast and left the house
usually about 6. Formerly he used the tube to and from
work; then he bought a Mini, but as he had no driving
licence yet, a non-Gujarati workmate drove him to and
from work, keeping the car overnight. He also acted as
a driving instructor.

At 7, his wife got up. She started the day ritually:
after bathing and 'washing her mouth' she addressed a
'slok' to Surya the sun-god. She made herself some food
and began to prepare breakfast for the lodgers.

The breakfast was traditionally English: egg and beans,
cornflakes or Weetabix, toast and marmalade.

The lodgers started getting up a little before 8, and came down to the kitchen for breakfast from about 8 till 9. After 9, Mrs Patel usually did not serve breakfast, but being a kind soul, her times were flexible.

Breakfast was taken in the kitchen. Unlike dinner, no one had a regular seat at the table.

There was seldom much conversation at breakfast, as people were still sleepy, and few were present at the same time. The talk at meals was in Gujarati or English. My impression was that some subjects tended to be talked about in English, jobs for example. Purely 'personal' talk was rather more often in Gujarati. I do not think that this differentiation was due only to my presence, but it is really difficult to say.

As this was an English meal, food was eaten in the English way, with knife, fork and spoon.

The lodgers then departed for their various places of work or study. Nobody went the same way, and they did not alter their routes so as to have company on the journey. All used public transport: bus stops and tube stations were conveniently close.

Usually at about 8.30, or more often a bit later, the two boys came down for their breakfast. If almost everyone else had finished, they would sit at the main table; if not, they went to a small table in the corner. At about 9 they rushed off to school; one was just around the corner and the other some ten minutes' walk away.

When everybody had left, the wife did the washing-up. Two days a week she went upstairs, once to change the sheets, and once to vacuum the rooms. If she needed any shopping, she did it then or immediately after lunch. A Gujarati grocer called every week (usually Saturday) with the provisions ordered by telephone. He did not often achieve the short chat he expected when he came, since (as I have mentioned) the owner of the house pushed him out firmly. The grocer's shop was roughly a mile away. When extra things were needed, the wife or more often the boys went to get them; they bought Indian groceries from a Punjabi shop near by and other things from the cheapest place they could find.

The wife would get lunch at home for the older boy, who said: 'The school lunch is bad, the food is no good.' His younger brother, however, stayed for lunch at school, as it was too far for him to return.

The afternoon and early evening were largely spent in preparing the dinner. This usually occupied at least four hours almost entirely. She spread this work out, however, by doing odd jobs in between.

Thus the preparation of purely Indian food involved a

good deal of additional time: one example was the preparation of poris. These were fried individually in deep fat
until 'they puffed up nicely', as one cooking book
describes it; since some eight to ten per person were
needed, and there were eleven people in the house, this
was a laborious task. And this process, carried out two
or three times a week (alternating with chapatties and
sweet chapatties), was only one of the many processes
involved in cooking one meal.

About 6 p.m. onwards, the lodgers began to return.
Dinner was at 7, and a bell was rung when it was ready.
Though one or two people were usually late for dinner,
having evening classes or overtime, all the rest would
usually come to the table at the same time. People
generally kept to the same seats, so this was an occasion
for a chat. The food was eaten in the traditional way,
using the right hand. Chapatties, poris or sweet
chapatties with shak and dal, and rice afterwards, was
the normal diet. There was a sweet on Sundays, usually
fresh fruit.

While Hindus and Jains strictly observed the distinction
in purity between left and right hand, the Muslims were
not so particular about this, though they did usually
follow the same rules. For them, I think, this had become
a custom rather than a strictly observed religious law.

Since the right hand is supposed to be cleaner than
the left, food should be taken up in the right hand only,
so as not to defile it. But touching the food makes that
hand unclean, so the left hand is used to help oneself
from trays and dishes, and to hold a glass of water or a
cup of tea.

To eat rice and dal, a spoon was sometimes used, but
more often by the Ismailis than by the others, who quite
often used their fingers. Neatly, moderately and with
well controlled and fairly slow movements was regarded
as the most proper way to eat. In the beginning I was
reprimanded for lifting my arm too much, and I still have
a feeling that in my Norwegian way - we regard fast eating
and rather 'energetic' movements as a sign of manliness
and a good healthy appetite - I really never learnt to
eat correctly.

I have said that there was a fair amount of general
talk at the dinner table about such topics as the latest
film shows, job prospects, shares, economic questions and
current affairs, and jokes about lots of things including
teasing Mrs Patel about marrying Patidar girls (the
supreme joke being about marrying her sister's daughter),
and one or two standard ones: that one of the Sudanese
boys was 'president of the literary society' in the Sudan

and that his father was a shipowner (but the Sudan has
no ships - Ha-Ha!). Another joke was to pour scorn on
the other person's place of origin. 'X? It's the worst
place in the world. Take my advice - never go there!'
(X was Mr Patel's home town.) I think that this atmosphere
of joking and relaxed talk was one of the attractions of
living in a Gujarati house.

This generally informal atmosphere was underlined by a
lack of formal greetings. Though 'Good morning' and
'Excuse me' were used, people usually simply said 'Hallo'.
Sometimes they would point out to me that this was one of
the main differences between staying in an English house
and in an Indian one.

After dinner, the lodgers returned to their rooms, or
sat watching TV for a while. If a popular programme was
on, more than the usual one or two would stay. About
this time, Mr Patel would return, and we know his
objections to the lodgers' monopolising the TV.

The family now had their own dinner. Mr and Mrs Patel
sometimes ate together, but the boys always ate separately.
When the couple do not eat at the same time, the man eats
before the wife. The Patels' table manners seemed to
resemble those of their Hindu and Jain lodgers.

The lodgers occasionally did not stay in in the evening,
and the two Ismailis often went out together, went out
more often, and spent more than the others. The others
would go singly or together, but never with the Ismailis.
The Jains and the Hindus mainly stayed in to work in the
evenings; Sundays were also occupied in study. Only
from 10 to 11 p.m. or so did they gather to hear some
Indian film music or chat.

The family, or at least the mother and father, went to
bed early, about 10 or 10.30. Mr Patel was often very
tired in the evening, and sometimes fell asleep immediately
after dinner. They would stay up a bit later if there was
a good television programme.

Mrs Patel expected the boys to go to bed about the same
time as she did, but they often stayed up to play for at
least another hour. Usually, however, they were in bed
before midnight.

This was the typical weekday domestic routine; Saturdays
and Sundays were different.

STRATEGIES LEADING OUT OF THE HOUSE

Mrs Patel's sister's daughter lived in the boys' room for
about a year. She later moved to her two brothers in a
different part of London, where she had her own room; she
was then living with even closer kin than before.

The graduate student went back to the Catholic hostel because of the climate for study – he said. Mr Patel never accepted this reason, and I was never clear about his true motive. The man was fussy about wanting too many different things for breakfast, the owner said, and he did not like him taking breakfast only.

Personally, I think that a conflict over rank was also involved. The graduate student regarded Mr Patel as someone interested only in money, and because of his education ˑresented the haughty way he was treated. This was most apparent when Mr Patel spoke to him. The owner, on his side, regarded the man who was still a student at forty as a no-good, I think, and here again we may see the conflict between the values of scholarship and those of business as a clue to why the graduate student moved out.

To the Ismaili students, as I have mentioned, Mr Patel's house was merely perhaps a stage in their continuing pursuit of independence: they themselves were quite specific about this.

One man lived in the house until he brought his family from East Africa. Then he moved into rented accommodation in the house of a Punjabi grocer some ten minutes away while he was looking for a house. He took his time, however, for as Mrs Patel said: 'Buying a house is difficult, and he wants nice house – see?' As they both went to work and had two children, however, they had problems, as was evident when they attempted to buy Indian food from Mr Patel to take away. This arrangement ceased to function, and the family then ate English food.

The form of Mr Patel's household and its relation to the main argument

This household form can, I think, be envisaged as a form of economic enterprise. In chapter 6, I was trying to say something about the purchase of the house in relation to Mr Patel's general economic strategies.

First, it may be said that he purposely chose a big house in order to be able to let rooms, and thus pay it off as quickly as possible. He criticized a caste fellow (N.T. Patel) for buying so small a house that there would be no rooms to let. 'How is he going to pay for his daughter's marriage?' Mr Patel said. (The daughter was, at that time, only five or six years old!)

He further chose to keep only two out of the seven rooms in the house for himself and his family. This might well be criticized on the grounds of other general values, for example one Ismaili student derided the way

Mr Patel was living. 'He could live like a company
manager', he said - the implication being that he ought
to be doing so. In addition, by letting rooms, he was
definitely in breach of his mortgage contract.

For Mr Patel, then, the house was maintained very much
as an integral part of his economic strategy. He was thus
economizing to a greater extent than would commonly be
accepted by members of the encompassing society. It is
by no means unusual for someone to buy a house and let
rooms as an integral part of the strategy of paying for
that house. But his degree of economizing, expressed as
the portion of the house being let, would, I think, be
rather frowned upon by members of the host society, and
it would certainly be exceptional. Within the bounds of
the encompassed society, however, people seemed to
conclude only that Mr Patel was really quite a good
businessman, and a fairly clever fellow, as he had
successfully evaded the restrictions in his mortgage
contract.

Other people were involved in the maintenance of such
a situation. One of the reasons why the Ismaili students
ultimately moved was that they did not fit into the ideal
of the 'good student'; another was that they disliked the
area. While it was cheap and convenient, it had certainly
not much status. It was evident from the comments of one
Ismaili that he thought it advisable to live in a good
house, as defined by the living standards of the owner,
even though he himself would have to lower his living
standards in other ways to afford the higher rent. He
was greatly taken with certain rooms he saw in the Golders
Green area, where the semi-detached houses are big and
beautiful and well set back in their gardens, and the
cars outside confirm the impression that the people living
there are indeed well off.

The four Sudanese students, on the other hand, were
not very much impressed by these considerations. They
referred very much more, in their talk, to their families
at home, and their views of what constituted a good
adaptation to London was coloured by the fact that they
did not want to be extravagant with the money they
received from their parents. But even the one who worked
full-time was more oriented than the Ismaili students
towards the 'good student' role ideal.

For the maintenance of such a role-play, then, Mr
Patel's house seemed quite suitable. It was cheap and
unassuming; and Indian food was served so that no caste
restrictions of diet had to be broken. The food was not
always praised, but the provision of meals enabled the
students to devote more time to their studies: they did

work hard. When they went out together they did not spend
freely, as the Ismailis did. They did not ask friends to
the house, and certainly not girls. The status of the
area therefore did not affect them.

In other words the ideal of economizing, the role ideal
of the 'good student' and the availability of the right
kind of food all contributed to make Mr Patel's house
attractive to these students. Though they were Banias,
and not a part of the encompassed Patidar community, I
believe that their behaviour in this respect very closely
resembled what could be called the Patidar norm of such
relationships.

The reasons the graduate student stayed on in the house
were probably the same as those of the four Sudanese
students. But he did not seem to have easily accepted
the inferior rank assigned to him by Mr Patel. In
conversations between the two, it seemed apparent that
the owner took it for granted that as the other was both
a lodger and a student, he ought to assume the position
of an inferior. He spoke to him accordingly, and it was
obviously resented. The graduate student continued to
address Mr Patel as an equal. I took over his room when
he moved back to the Catholic hostel where he had been
staying before, which seemed to give him both the cheap-
ness and the respectability necessary in order to keep up
the 'good student' image.

I think, therefore, that the strategies leading the
various lodgers into Mr Patel's house can be seen as
highly compatible with their general strategies and with
the value orientations outlined above. Consequently, it
makes sense to see the household, in this case, as a
social form resulting from adaptation to the encompassed
type of situation I have been discussing.

The other example of a household with lodgers is
Tusharbhai's flat (Figure 14). Here, too, a nuclear
family forms the core. For some time the year before
Tusharbhai's father had been staying there. At the time
of my stay, there were the following lodgers. First,
there was an old Patidar who worked for Tusharbhai in his
firm. Further, there was a young Patidar woman, who was
a village-fellow of Tusharbhai's wife, and whose family
lived outside London (Tara Patel). She did a good deal
of the housework as well as being a lodger. A young
Lohana was a lodger in the house, as was Kumar, a Patidar
working as a clerk, and me (A). We two shared a room,
the other lodgers had single rooms. Unlike the lodgers
in Anilbhai's house, the lodgers in this house was
practically treated as family members. I have reason to
believe, however, that this was fairly atypical. In this

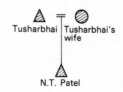

(1) cooks the food   A = anthropologist

FIGURE 14   Tusharbhai's household

household, it may be said that the lodgers, especially
Tara Patel, were treated as junior relatives (as Tara
Patel almost was).

STRATEGIES LEADING INTO TUSHARBHAI'S HOUSEHOLD

I have told Tusharbhai's own story in a previous chapter.
It was only when his business led him to London that he
started looking for a flat. If his business had not been
so centrally located, he might have preferred to buy a
house. Now a primary factor in his choice was to
minimize the distance to the shop. Otherwise, he wanted
plenty of room and generally a nice place. He looked
at quite a few flats in the area before he settled for
this one. He indicated to me that taking lodgers had
not been an initial consideration, but he had taken this
up in order to pay for his sister's wedding. This was
described by 'India Weekly' as the wedding of the year:
the dowry was alleged to be in the region of between
£3,000 and £4,000, and the wedding itself was no cheap
affair either, as about 1,000 guests ('India Weekly's'
estimate) were present.
     For the intellectual middle-class Londoner, a flat in
the middle of London - in this case not far from either
the University area or from Soho - seems to be a popular
housing alternative. Judging also from how Tusharbhai
had furnished his house, with a secure taste and
simplicity very different from the charming but rather
flowery style common among most Patidar immigrants - his
general conception of good living was probably influenced
a lot by upper-middle class intellectual standards. One

Indian student friend of mine, hearing where I lived,
jokingly remarked, 'Oh, very trendy!' and this seemed
typical. He himself was a very radical man who would
have nothing to do with middle-class intellectualism.

The old Patidar mentioned clearly owed his presence
in the household to his general relation of clientship to
Tusharbhai, which, as stated above, was based on his
working in the firm. No further explanation is necessary
here.

Tara Patel had come to London from the small provincial
town where her father lived in order to do a certain job,
connected with a trade in which she had a great interest.
It is not common for Patidar girls to stay away from home
unless they have male relatives to look after them. Tara
Patel's parents allowed her to stay in London specifically
because she stayed with a man who, while he was not strictly
speaking a relative, was well known to them and had a
reputation as somebody of a high ethical character.

The young Lohana was not working for Tusharbhai
and thus came fairly close to being a 'pure lodger'. The
convenient location as well as the nice atmosphere may
account for his presence.

Kumar, the young Patidar clerk, had come from East
Africa, but his old father was still living in Charottar.
His greatest interest was in music and theatre, and he
clearly enjoyed living in the centre of London where
these interests might effectively be pursued. He had a
brother in south London, but preferred to live with
Tusharbhai, partly because of the location, partly because
of the artistic interests of his host, and partly because
of the freedom enjoyed by living with non-relatives.
Here, he could more easily live the life of an artisti-
cally interested metropolitan.

A day in Tusharbhai's household

It is considerably more difficult to give a general
picture of an 'ordinary day' in this household. In fact,
the most striking difference between the two households
was exactly the relative monotony of Anilbhai and his
lodgers contrasted with the much more changing and
diversified life here. This relates directly to the work
of the heads of the households. While Anilbhai had his
fixed working hours to keep up, Tusharbhai's shop was not
his only care. Instead, he had to look after his song-
and-dance society as well as numerous other economic and
artistic ventures. One day, therefore, he would leave to
meet some business associate; the next day a meeting might
take place in his living-room.

But apart from this, it is possible to get a general
idea. Both Tusharbhai and his wife got up early, both
going to work in the business. Breakfast would not be
eaten all together, but food would be left for the lodgers,
who would then get up and breakfast as their diverse needs
directed. The breakfast here consisted of chapatties or
pori, tea, and usually left-overs from the previous day's
dinner. Usually, the next to get up would be the old man,
Tara Patel and the young Lohana, leaving Kumar and myself
to get up last.   The young son of the owner would go
to the shop to be tended there in between shopkeeping
duties. An agile and quick little boy, he was the main
amusement of the household, everybody taking turns to
look after him.   Tara Patel would usually return first,
cooking the dinner and serving the lodgers separately
as they returned from work.   Dinner was not taken at
a fixed time.   Quite often the owner and his wife,
returning late from work, would be the last to eat.
Later, if there was not a business meeting, everybody
would gather in the living room talking and watching the
TV. A pleasant atmosphere was enjoyed, quite a lot of
joking going on, and the little boy continuously amusing
us.
     The lodgers, in this house, clearly felt much less like
lodgers, and there was a family atmosphere involving
everybody.

The form of this household and its relation to the main
argument

This household form differs materially from that of
Anilbhai, as to its inhabitants. The owner as well as
some of the lodgers might be said to belong to the fringe
group of intellectual middle-class Indians in London
rather than to the community of ordinary immigrants. Yet
this would be a false assumption, for they are members
equally of both. It is not difficult to see the advantage
of taking lodgers, but, on the other hand, this is not
something the owner has always done. In fact he chose,
during the first years of his tenancy, to avoid it. The
flat, then, does not seem to be chosen with this end
primarily in view. Closeness to his shop as well as the
general convenience and standard of the flat seems to
have been more important. It is interesting that, in
spite of this, he had still decided to take lodgers.
     In the form of the household, even more, perhaps, than
in that of Anilbhai, we see the shadow of the joint
family. It is present both in the general familiarity and

warmth of the atmosphere and in the care of the child. The rooms were not 'private' as they were in Anilbhai's house, and everybody felt free to use the kitchen and the living room as they saw fit - it was not a case of 'intruding'.

The lodgers were all rather special people. The cultural interests of the owner was shared by them and contributed to the general feeling of cosmopolitanism.

This example shows, I think, that the patterns described from Anilbhai's household, and the strategies generating that pattern, are found among middle-class Patidars as well. At the same time, it shows that, while a great deal of cultural diversity may be found within the Patidar community, contacts are maintained across any 'barrier' created by these differences.

OTHER HOUSEHOLDS

Perhaps obviously, I did not have the chance to live in a pure family household taking no lodgers. I therefore have to describe the family type of household in a much more fragmented fashion. From visits made, however, I have reason to believe that ritual and customs from home were, if anything, more copiously followed in these households than as I have described in Anilbhai's. The tulsi plant and the images - usually of Laxmi and Ghanshyam - were generally omni-present. When tea was served it was always of the Gujarati type, made from boiling milk. The food I was served with when visiting was always Indian, except for things like biscuits.

N.T. Patel's house is a typical family house (Figure 15). Beside the nuclear family, N.T.'s brother, who was studying for the GCE, lived in the house. He paid no rent and was thus definitely a junior relative, as might be expected.

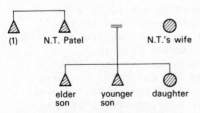

(1) a young boy studying for his GCE

FIGURE 15   N.T. Patel's household

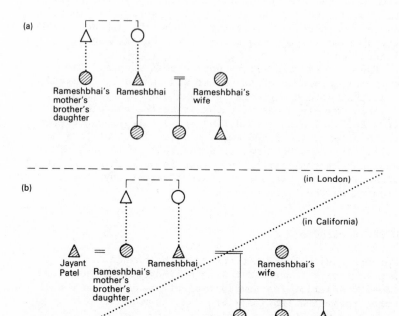

FIGURE 16   Rameshbhai's household at two stages

Rameshbhai's house, at the first stage (Figure 16a) had a similar set-up. Again, to a nuclear family was added one 'junior relative'. She was a mother's brother's daughter of Rameshbhai.

Of course, there were also households which were exclusively nuclear family households. For any idea of numerical proportions as between different types of households, my data is regrettably much too scarce.

In Figure 16b I have illustrated a pattern which is more unusual. This represents Rameshbhai's household when I left Britain. At that time, he had sent wife and children to America, and had married off his junior relative. The London house therefore now consisted of Rameshbhai, his mother's brother's daughter, and her husband, Jayant Patel. The part of Rameshbhai's household who were in American were staying with relatives, but I do not know what kind of relatives.

There was another example of such a 'divided' household among my informants, that of Harishbhai (Figure 17).

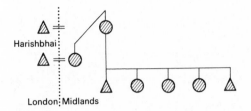

FIGURE 17 Harishbhai's two households

Essentially, this household consisted of Harishbhai's
nuclear family living in the Midlands, with the exception
of himself, who lived and worked in London. With
Harishbhai's wife, however, was staying her sister, while
the sister's husband lived in London with Harishbhai (in
the same house, but in two single rooms).

The examples of 'divided' households may go to show
the elasticity of the form of households among the Patidar
community. In pursuing certain strategies, re-organization of the household may become necessary, and it seems
that the authority of the husband remains strong enough
to ensure that such re-organization takes place. In
some cases the wives spoke to me of their regret in this
matter, but did not seem to have many sanctions at their
disposal.

These examples may all be seen as variations of the
nuclear family household. However, brothers may also
share a flat or a house. Examples of this are the flats
occupied by the households shown in Figures 18 and 19.

A question presenting itself is this: is there any
tendency for joint-family households to form in Britain?
I do not think this question can be adequately answered
from my data. What is clear is, first, that siblings and
other relatives sometimes do combine in forming a household. It does not seem to be usual, on the other hand,
for more than one nuclear family to be found in the same
household; what I found was generally either a nuclear

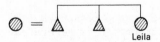

FIGURE 18 The household where Leila lives

FIGURE 19

family with one or more 'junior relatives' - usually
single - attached, or two or three siblings residing
together, all of whom might as yet be unmarried. In the
case of the household shown in Figure 19, the man brought
his wife into the flat after the two brothers had already
been living there for some time. These sibling groups,
then, tended to consist of fairly young people (perhaps
up to 30 years of age).

It remains, then, unclear whether it is convenient to
designate any of the households mentioned as 'joint'.
That being said, however, there certainly are some traits
of the joint family present. What I mean by saying this
is that, first, there seems to be no strong resistance
for people from different nuclear families to live
together. On the other hand, there seems to be some
preference for a large household. This preference may
be related directly to the character of the houseowner/
lodger and the houseowner/junior relative relationship
as described above. For the houseowner, heading a large
household means having dependents and thus gives prestige.
For him, therefore, there is a definite advantage in
having as large a household as he can manage. For the
junior relatives, living in the house means that they are
not quite regarded as socially independent. This is
probably quite acceptable to a relative who is really
junior, as is, for example, N.T. Patel's brother, being
probably about 15 years younger than his host. For a
married man with family such acceptance may be more
difficult. This may explain why I did not find more than
one complete nuclear family in one household at a time
among my informants - which does not mean that it may not
exist.

The variety of household forms suggest that households
should not be analysed as 'types' but rather as generated
from the strategies of their members (compare Pehrsson,
1966, pp.86-99), as I have tried to do above regarding
the households of Anilbhai and Tusharbhai.

Let us turn again to Figure 11 above. The points in

this value conversion where consideration of household forms is relevant can be summarized as follows:

1 As long as the actor's only resource is his time, used as wage-labour, he may be supposed mainly to be interested in minimizing household costs for himself. Living as a partner or as a junior relative in a larger household would then be ideal. For single students, much the same is true.

2 If he has got some capital himself at this stage, he can convert this into a regular income by buying a house and letting rooms, alone or in partnership. He might prefer people somehow related to him as lodgers, since they might more easily become his dependants.

Actors in these two stages would combine to form bachelor-houses.

3 At some point, one of the members of such a household might marry or bring his wife to Britain.

4 If he is then owner or co-owner, some of the lodgers or junior relatives would be asked to move, so as to make room for the family. If the house is small, he might need all of it.

5 If he is himself a lodger or a junior relative, he might have to be content with very cramped quarters, and would try to find something bigger, either on his own, or in partnership with others.

6 The owner now has to make a decision. If he chooses to ask them to move and to keep the other lodgers, he may make more money.

7 If the first alternative is chosen, we may get a household almost like a joint family. It can, for our purpose here, be seen as the outcome of strategies maximizing prestige. In some ways, Tusharbhai's household approximated to this.

8 If the second alternative is chosen, we may get a household almost like a lodging-house. Anilbhai's household - as in Figure 13 - is a case of this.

9 Since the above is a basic dilemma in the formation of Patidar households in London, not only the composition, but also the style of role-play in households are related to it; see 'The Houseowner and his Lodger' above.

10 This dilemma is related to the general dilemma, as emerges from Figure 11, of allocating one's resources to gain cash or prestige, respectively.

11 Prestige of this kind is dependent upon values - related to kin obligations and dependence - quite different from those of the encompassing society. Cash, in this case, is also related to encompassment in that it is generally cheaper to live in a Gujarati house. This is certainly true for junior relatives, and to some extent,

because of the food, for the lodgers too. And it is
certainly true for the owners, because of the rent.
   The household forms described can therefore be seen
as important for the maintenance of an 'encompassed
Patidar community'.
   It seems to me that the influx of refugees from Uganda
after 1972 might have resulted in a considerable increase
in the number of available lodgers or, by definition,
dependents. During visits to east London non-Patidar
Indian households in 1975, and conversations with social
workers there, cases of houseowners wishing to get rid
of such lodgers were, it seems, now not unusual. If such
is indeed the case, I would take it to mean that the
patron-client relationship implicit in the householder-
lodger relationship is, in these cases, breaking up.
While formerly, and as described in this book, such
relationships were instrumental in integrating the
community - keeping even those who did not quite live up
to Patidar standards within it - it is quite possible
that by now poor, jobless lodgers are excluded.
   These households, then, are connected by ties of
kinship, village origin, caste, and to a much lesser
extent friendship across these lines, usually contracted
in England. These ties are not substantially different
from those linking households in London to households
outside the capital. Marriage circles should also be
counted among the factors active in creating such ties.
   Such ties are, moreoever, not confined to the Patidar
community in Britain. Ties of this kind link all Patidar
communities together, whether they be in India, in East
Africa or in any other part of the world. In this way,
the Patidars' idea of themselves as a world-wide
community of businessmen has some basis in the truth.
   Because such ties exist, no Patidar, even if his
household is the only one in a particular town, is really
isolated. He will be in contact with relatives in his
home village, and with emigrants from that village in
other parts of the world. Matrilateral kin or affinals
also form part of his network, whether they are in Britain
or not. But due to their dispersal practical considerations and personal likings will, in individual cases, be
decisive as to which of these ties the actor chooses to
stress.
   This clearly has implications for 'integration'. The
Patidar who is alone in settling in a certain town may
still be looking to his kin and village contacts rather
than to the local population for personal contacts and
for help in practical matters. Thus there is no need to
regard physical dispersal of the community as something

conducive to integration into the encompassing society.

Patidar communities, in London or even in Britain as a whole, are encompassed within British society. This encompassment follows from the fact that the territorial unit is taken as the frame of reference. If a world-wide perspective was adopted, Britain and other ecological settings would be contained within Patidar society as a whole, namely as bases for different settlements within the - in principle - world-wide caste.

Settlements in Britain thus form but one section of all the Patidar settlements, just as the different settlements in Britain should be seen as parts of the all-British Patidar community.

London, however, ranks above the other settlements in Britain, and this was most clearly evident when I tried to find contacts outside London. Asking people whether they had any contacts in the north, for example, got me no response whatsoever. Only after I had lived in Coventry for some time did the same people tell me that I had gone to the wrong place: if I had gone to Huddersfield or Leeds instead, they would have arranged for me to stay with friends or relatives there. I do think that this reflects the fact that the north was regarded as a rather 'low' area, and one did not know people there. Likewise, one did not want a friend (as I assume myself to be) to go to such a place.

In London the different areas are unequally ranked too, but this generally fits the English view of the place in question. The only exception is that places like Hampstead, so full of associations to the English or in fact the European intellectual, has no such appeal to the Patidars. Likewise, Golders Green is perhaps seen as rather nouveau-riche by the English higher classes. The Patidars, being, if successful, rather nouveau-riche themselves, do not seem to take this into account.

This does not mean that the drabness of the areas where most Patidars live is not recognized by them. A temple situated in Camden Town was said to be in a 'bad' area, and the committee dearly wished that with increased funds it would become possible to move.

I have said that there is little organization beyond the household. The existence of temples and cultural associations do, however, form an important exception. But most of the people go to the functions for entertainment, and though some go for more explicitly religious reasons, few indeed take any interest in the internal

politics of these associations. There may be, in some
cases, a core of people going to one temple or association,
but the people I met did not generally 'belong' to a
temple even in this sense. There were, however, some
indications that this might be changing. Certainly while
I was there people who had not been to a temple for years
suddenly started going, and people who, some time before,
had clearly gone only for entertainment now went with
enthusiasm and gave money. Thus, Veenabhai, my landlord's
wife, did in fact begin to participate in some ritual:
she was allowed to worship the village 'Mata' (village-
goddess) in the nearby Swaminarayana temple.

This temple, by the way, was probably the only one
which had real funds, and was in part the work of the
'top leader'.

Let me describe briefly the opening of this temple.
This took place on 14 June 1970. A procession was staged,
walking from Hyde Park Corner to the temple. The attendance
was estimated to be as high as 1,500. A 'temple chariot'
in the form of a decorated lorry led the way. Yogiji
Maharaj, the present leader of the sect and an incarnation
of the founder, led the way. He was followed by a company
of monks from Gujarat, dressed, like himself, in orange
robes. It was a splendid sight. The 'top leader' was
very much in charge of the practical operations. The
temple was furnished with chairs painted in gold for the
occasion. The building itself, an old church hall, had
been painted in blue and orange and stood out in the dark
street like a flower among stones. After the official
opening, to which all the notables were invited, the
people were bussed to an older temple in Camden Town for
a free meal.

At the new meeting at 5 o'clock, the 'top leader'
spoke, as did the High Commissioner of India, Lord
Sorensen, the Lord Mayor of the Borough of Islington, and
a learned follower of the faith. A speech by His Highness
Yogiji Maharaj, translated into English, had been taped
and was presented to the audience.

After this meeting, the first satsang, i.e. the first
'communion' meeting, was held. For this the chairs were
removed and the speeches were now held in Gujarati. 'We
were left in Darkness, but Swami came with the Light' and
'We were like children with no parents in London, but now
Bapu [Father] has come' were among the themes of these
speeches.

There were many speeches, and people spoke from where
they stood, reminding the author slightly of Christian
revival meetings, but at last His Highness spoke himself.
The monks chanted, whereas the audience clapped their

hands for rhythm. One man stood forward singing a song
he himself had made in honour of His Highness. Then the
images - that of Shree Swaminarayana himself in the
middle - were fed, and prasad - the holy meal - was
distributed to the audience. This is the satsang or
'communion' itself. It was a solemn and very beautiful
occasion.

The satsang was, of course, the institutionalized
ritual of the temple, and takes place every night. Some
people also come for morning prayers. Sundays are the
most active days.

His Highness and his company stayed on for some time,
and this, of course, made for an even greater attendance
than that which was seen later. However, people did not
seem to lose interest when he had gone. Rather, a basis
for a large stable audience to the temple seemed to have
been laid.

During the first four weeks after the opening of the
temple, a course for writing and reading Gujarati was
also held in the temple.

After the departure of His Highness and his company,
the temple was left in the care of a middle-aged man 'in
the status of householder', i.e. a man in the third
stage of the ideal Hindu life cycle.

I should mention here that the day after the opening
of the temple the 'top leader' was present in the temple
receiving gifts to the institution and giving advice to
people. Advice might be given on a number of things,
like, 'What shall I call my son who has just been born?'
The anthropologist asked for advice on his fieldwork.
It was the common thing to prostrate oneself in front
of the leader when asking advice, as when a Guru is
approached in India.

As will be evident from this short description, I do
not here attempt to undertake a study of ritual as such
in the temples. What I am trying to show is that the
temple is a setting which makes a revival of numerous
forms of behaviour from the home context possible. This
is not at all restricted to religion. The use of the
language on a public occasion, as well as sitting on the
floor, behaving towards people present in Britain like
one does to an Indian Guru, all this helps to keep alive
forms which otherwise might have fallen into disuse.
That this makes people feel at home is evident. The
atmosphere in the temple is far from the sinister gravity
of church-going among Westerners. People joke and enjoy
themselves. Thus, one evening the text was read by a
young boy who had evident difficulties with reading
Gujarati, difficulties hardly relieved by nervousness.

After he had finished, an elderly, good-humoured fellow
broke out: 'Well, he has passed the exam, hasn't he?'
('Periksha pas theyo, nehi?') and people laughed good-
heartedly.

The dividing line between temples and associations was
almost impossible to draw. This may be undergoing a
change, as more 'specialized' temples come into existence.
The Swaminarayana temples - there were two of them - were
such specialized temples, and did not generally involve
themselves in non-religious activity. The other associations might deal with quite a range of cultural activity.
All the activity, however, was conspicuously non-political,
thus reflecting the general feeling in the community that
'politics are dirty stuff'. No temple or association was
exclusively Patidar.

        There was, however, some indications that internal
political issues were about to be brought into this
sector. This manifested itself in the differences between
a national organization of the cultural associations in
many towns, an organization which was led by the editor
of the Gujarati paper, and which stressed the maintenance
of Gujarati culture and language in Britain. This was in
theory as well as in practice a multi-caste organization.
On the other hand, there was the London-based organization
led by Sarobhai Patel. This organization used English
in all its communications and tried to embrace people
from all parts of India. In fact, however, the membership
was, according to Sarobhai Patel himself, about 80 per
cent Patidar.

        Sarobhai Patel's story of the origin of his organiza-
tion may be of interest. Sarobhai Patel himself is a
Patidar who, after finishing his studies at Poona,
settled first in Bombay and then in East Africa, where
he started his own insurance business. When he came to
England he set himself up in the same line, operating in
south London.

        The organization was started in the autumn of 1969.
'It suddenly struck me what was the position of the
Indians in this country. The children here do not want
to forget Indian traditions. So I discussed these things
with my wife, and with friends. The contacts with
neighbours, in India, had to be replaced by an organization. I did lots of labour, but after fifteen years I
had recruited fifty members. I chose the president and
the vice-president: the rest of the Committee was elected.
The organization should act as a colordinator, in such a
way that British people could learn about Indian culture.

Fifteen out of the thirty people I asked became patrons,
paying £15 each. Nomination fees were put at fifty pence
per year. Soon there were 200 members for everybody in
the Committee. Let's see if I will be successful.'

The organization has an official circular. At the
opening, a hall taking 500 had been let, but several
thousands, according to Sarobhai Patel, turned up. This
was in October 1969.

There was another function in November, then a free
show of Indian dances, and then a great communal dinner
for 350-450 peopoe.

Other functions followed, and soon press reports were
published 'as far as France'. Sarobhai Patel was asked
to stage a TV programme, but decided to wait. For the
Queen's birthday a great celebration in her honour was
held. The progtammes were arranged by Tusharbhai's
organization. The Queen herself was invited, as were a
number of English notables. The Queen, unhappily, was
unable to come.

'The Indian community still has its problems. We have
the "culture", but we do not have the facilities. One
important thing is that we have now got an Indian firm
renting out cooking utensils and other material for the
arrangement of functions, able to cater for up to 3,000
people.

'But it is lots of hard work. I was about to resign
last month, but they forced me not to. All the Gujarati
organizations have been joining me lately. And there is
a certain exchange of culture: three English girls are
now taking up Indian dancing. After all, this is our
home land. We are British now.'

I asked him about the large number of Patidars on the
committee. Did this mean that the organization was,
essentially, a Patidar one?

'No,' he said. 'The organization is open to all
Hindus. But since I started with my friends, naturally
they were Patels. They got their friends to join, and
so it spread. It is true that there are many Patidars
on the committee. But there are many others [non-
Patidars] as members.'

'What about the organization of the editor from
Surat?' I asked. 'It is a different set-up. We are
trying to maintain Hindu unity. Therefore, all our
material is in English. We also do have some English
course activity.'

The organization of the editor from Surat is, indeed,
a different set-up. It is not, in fact, one organization,
but rather an association of the different local organizations, all with a cultural and religious basis, which
are found throughout the country.

Two of these organizations are described in Desai
(1963, pp.108-21) and personally I know them from visits
to Rugby (where I was kindly taken by the editor) and
from Coventry.

Usually their main activity centres around ritual.
This includes 'secular' as well as 'sacred' ritual as it
covers the celebration of occasions such as Republic Day.
In Rugby a certain hall was let by the organization every
Sunday. In Coventry, through the activities of the local
organization as well as a local Catholic priest, an old
disused school had been placed at the disposal of the
organization. These associations seems to be, in general,
very explicitly non-sectarian in their practice of
Hinduism, though, as in Gujarat, the Vaishnavist influence
is very strong on local religion.

The editor had this to say about the formation of the
association: 'I was helping to found the association. I
met most of the leaders - the office-holders - of those
organizations while trying to spread the circulation of
the paper. So I tried to convince them that they should
unite, and they agreed to do so.'

In relation to Sarobhai Patel's set-up, he had this to
say: 'Our association has not joined his set-up. Neither
is that a member of the association. It would then have
to approve of the decisions of the association. His
organization is for a small part of the country only,
whereas the association has members all over the country.'

'It seems that his organization is almost 80 per cent
Patidar?' I asked.

'Oh yes, that is true.'

'But none of the honorary members of the association
are Patidars - is that significant?'

'Well, there is no Patidar among the honorary members,
but there are many Patidar members throughout the country.'

'We believe', he continued, 'in Gujarati language. It
is important to keep the own language, for the culture
cannot exist without the language.'

His newspaper, of course, is of great help here. The
editor himself, not a Patidar, comes from Surat district.
Besides his own newspaper, he is the London correspondent
of two important Gujarati newspapers.

This difference in emphasis - the all-Hindu, English-
speaking approach, and the Gujarati, Gujarati-speaking
approach, would merit a further study. It is evident
that a situation like the one we are describing offers
numerous alternative strategies for political entrepreneurship (see Eidheim, 1963, passim). The two organizations described here may be seen as alternative
solutions to the general problem of maintaining cultural

identity and ethnic separateness in a foreign setting.
The job to be done - the task that both these leaders see
clearly before them - is one of instituting a suitable
form for expression of the ethnic identity, a form which
fits the framework set by the encompassing society. The
language dilemma clearly is a classic one in such
situations (see Eidheim, 1963).

The 'top leader', in commenting upon these organizations,
did see some bright points but generally lamented the lack
of leadership in this, as in all, Commonwealth immigrant
communities. He was confident, however, that 'leadership
will emerge'. In the light of the activity going on
during my stay, I tend to agree. What he saw as important
was to find a solution to the dilemma of identity: 'We
must become British Gujaratis without becoming Brown
Englishmen.'

As a political entrepreneur he was evidently the one
who had done best, and his services seemed to be of a
great and lasting importance to the community. His
emphasis that 'the minorities must stick together' was
borne out by his own position, where he, in many cases,
represented the Commonwealth immigrants as a whole as
against British bureaucracy.

Membership of associations like these was not very
widespread, and even so, very few among the members took
any part in running them.

I should perhaps finally mention the astrologer, who was
quite an institution all by himself. He used to be a
businessman but had left the business to his wife and
his solicitors and had become a sanyasi (a holy man).
He was an astrologer, and at the same time he had pledged
to devote a steadily increasing part of his time to
prayers for world peace. He really merits a thesis all
by himself, but I only mention him here to show that
there is a need for the services of an astrologer among
Patidars and other Indians in London, and to show that
the Hindu idea of settling down to seek moksha (enlighten-
ment) after an active life is very much alive in the
community. He was greatly respected, even by people who
may not have liked him or may even have thought that he
was not a very precise astrologer. He also did a large
amount of work for non-Indians.

This this is not an isolated instance is perhaps
illustrated by the fact that the leader of the Coventry
community - a community consisting of numerous castes -
had also, in a similar way, renounced his business,
turning to religion and the pursuit of moksha.

There are other astrologers in London, some only practising as a hobby. This is but one instance of a general tendency. This, as an example of the survival of Indian-ness, bears out what Desai described as the Indians' wish to accommodate to rather than to integrate into British society (Desai, 1963, p.147). This tendency is for the Patidar and other Indian communities to establish their own way of life in Britain. This does not mean reconstructing an Indian village on foreign soil, but it does mean that the character of the communities they create is very specifically Indian.

I shall discuss this and other themes further in my conclusion.

8 Conclusion

In concluding my arguments I shall keep to the specific analysis of the London Patidars as a case in the study of urban ethnicity, and only when that has been done, shall I turn to some more general comments.

I started off by presenting the London Patidars as people to whom making money and presenting a 'merchant' identity to the world is extremely important. I used the term 'merchant ideology' to describe this scale for evaluation of alternatives for action.

I tried to show that this ideology has its roots in Gujarati society itself, and that the 'merchant ideology' of the Patidars might be regarded as just one case of a caste imitating the castes which stand at the apex of the local hierarchy. In Africa this ideology was further strengthened since there the Patidars did in fact constitute a community of traders and white-collar employees.

Then I turned to Britain, viewed as an ecological setting for immigrants. I tried to show, very briefly, the range of opportunities open to them in work and housing.

The rest of the book, then, may be regarded as an analysis of the specific adaptation of the Patidars in this setting.

It was to describe this specific adaptation that I introduced the terms 'encompassed community' and 'encompassing society'. By using these terms the maintenance of the ethnic boundary between the Patidars and the society surrounding them was put in focus.

This was done by describing, first, the social structure of economic transactions that emerges when looking at the community. Next, strategies of a few individuals were singled out, and the form which emerges from the inter-action of people following strategies like these was briefly described.

125

To analyse the maintenance of the ethnic boundary from this presentation of the data I shall look at it from two points of view simultaneously.

The first is that of economic action. I have tried to show that the strategies followed by the Patidars make sense economically. They are, in fact, doing rather well.

The second point of view is that of ideology. I am thinking here first and foremost of the ideas concerning ethnic separateness and the ideas Patidars entertain about the relation between their own immigrant community and the larger society.

The question asked from these two points of view simultaneously is one and the same; how does it come about that there is such an 'encompassed community', in so many ways distinct from the larger society, rather than just individual households trying to make their way in British society in the same way and entertaining the same attitudes as the British themselves?

In asking this question, I am rejecting the idea that such an 'encompassed community' forms just one stage in the assimilation of immigrants. I am rejecting as insufficient the explanation that since these people are different they naturally act differently from their 'hosts' in the new setting. I am seeking an explanation in terms of why it is - or seems - rational to the Patidars to act as they do, and why they find their ideas about the relation between the larger society and themselves confirmed by experience.

In many ways, the questions as well as the answers are very similar to those put by Abner Cohen in his analysis of 'retribalization' among the Hausa in Yoruba towns in Nigeria (Cohen, 1969, passim). The differences are mainly in the use of certain terms, in that I am trying to make use of Barth's 'generative models' in my analysis (Barth, 1966, passim). In following this line of analysis - I concentrate more on the individual actors' choices, and concomitantly I am not relying to the same extent on historical material. When I use macro-data, I am trying to pinpoint where they impinge on the strategies of individual actors, as restrictions on their choices.

In seeking an explanation as to why the individual Patidar acts as he does, I am trying to show that his actions are understandable as being economically rational. In doing so, I have to take as given his own view of his position vis-à-vis the encompassing society, as well as the restrictions that the economic conditions prevailing in British capitalist society lay upon him.

In seeking an explanation of why he thinks as he does about the relation between his own caste-fellows and the

society, I am trying to show that these ideas are confirmed
daily by his experiences in England. I am accepting that
some of his ideas are rooted in his background, but I
assume that if they did not tally with experience they
would soon change.

It can generally be said for the Patidars studied that
the consumption takes place within a frame of reference
describable as an encompassed immigrant society. The
values according to which he defines himself, and according
to which the relevant others ascribe him his rank, are
therefore distinct from and largely different from those
of the encompassing society.

Also, it is within the frames of reference of the
encompassed society that a certain job is ascribed rank;
this ranking may therefore differ from that of the
encompassing society. In the Patidar case, it does; such
rank criteria as working in a well-established firm or in
some solid bureaucracy does not seem to be highly valued;
whereas a salesman may be judged very highly on the simple
measure that he takes home more money. This seems to
reflect a certain difference in evaluation from the
standards current in British society.

In so far as the businessman is selling his produce to
members of the encompassing society, this remains true.
Here also, the investment in capital and labour is placed
in something the businessman looks upon only as an
economic niche. In this it differs from at least a
considerable portion of the encompassing society's own
businessmen, who at least share their basic social values
with their customers. Members of the encompassed society,
on the other hand, will be given preferential treatment,
either in price reductions or, more commonly, in that the
shop will be open to them at any time as long as the
shopkeeper is at home.

As I have said before, the consumption of earnings
takes place in an environment dominated by the values of
the encompassed society. Some idea of these values have
already been given in the part of this book concerning
itself with the background of the Patidars. I shall here
take as given, therefore, the predominance of 'merchant'
values, the positive ranking of a 'merchant-like' job, and
the view of Patidar identity as essentially the identity
of a businessman.

It is clear, then, that within this framework these
values give satisfaction mainly to those who show themselves capable of actually making money. It is clear,
also, that in the light of these values, the job of
salesman is given higher rank than that of factory worker.
The people to whom the values of the encompassed society

bring the greatest satisfaction – or better, the people
whose actions are more in accordance with these values –
are therefore, at the same time, those who succeed in
making more money than the rest and for this reason also
command greater resources.

In one case, a factory worker was married to the wife's
brother's daughter of a very successful salesman. At the
wedding the worker's friends complained that the
arrangements were not all that they should have been, and
at more than one occasion later the son-in-law told me
that he felt treated as a very junior person by his in-
laws. 'He is treating me like a brother's son, not like
a son-in-law,' he said, the former term implying a more
junior position. When the father-in-law discussed diverse
business opportunities with his friends, thus communica-
ting his and their business capabilities and initiative,
the son-in-law remained silent. But he lived in his
father-in-law's house and could hardly complain directly;
neither does he ever challenge the ideal of business
capability, which obviously seems to be the ideological
background to his debased rank.

Earlier I noted that there are indications that, due
to the large number of people expelled from Uganda in
1972, the number of lodgers available as dependents has
exceeded the amount that houseowners can – or will –
absorb. In terms of unemployed members of the community,
a similar process may today be taking place. Thus, one
might expect that jobless Patidars, who in 1971 were still
taken care of by more fortunate members of the community
until they could support themselves, may now be too many
for the patron-client ties to keep them within the
community. This, at the present stage, is but a guess
founded in information from social workers in east London,
but as a hypothesis it seems to fit well into the analysis
of the community's social structure as presented in this
book.

It is my theory that kinship links, even when much less
definite than in this case, make it difficult for any
member of the encompassed society to challenge the
ideology of that society without breaking kinship
obligations. Also, there is no obvious alternative.
There are, obviously, people who drop out from the
encompassed society, attempting integration, but in the
cases I have encountered the persons involved had
academic education (one a librarian, the other an engineer)
and had secured for themselves good jobs within British
institutions. They were therefore dropouts because of
their independence, rather than as a reaction against
dependence (though the engineer was extremely unhappy

about the conflict between his own western-ness and his parents' conservatism.)

But the power of the encompassed society's ideals - as held up by its leading members - are not just coercive. They also constitute for even the poorest of the society's members, first, an ideology claiming the possibility of success - substantiated by the fact that the more successful community members have amassed considerable savings in a few years - the potential success therefore seems realistically attainable to everybody, and second, the ideology of saving means that the community member finds his reference group willing to accept a low standard of living as legitimate - he is not, therefore, as he might be in the encompassing society, socially sanctioned in a negative manner for lack of status symbols. Saving and a low level of spending are in themselves to some extent status symbols. It is only after a considerable time that it will become clear to others whether he has been saving money or whether he just hasn't been able to earn much.

Also, as long as he sees himself as external to the encompassing society, and as moving around on his own initiative in order to gain in income rather than as participating in the career patterns of the encompassing society, he will need a foundation in the encompassed society to legitimize his movement as well as to assist him materially when moving.

The choice between the encompassed society and the encompassing society's standards is therefore a vital one. Only if he has ample reason to believe that he can make it on his own within the encompassing society, backed up by such resources as money or education, is he likely to take this step.

However, as noted earlier, there may be certain members of the community who, by exceeding the numbers of lodgers and clients that the houseowners or patrons are willing to take on, are 'dropping out' of the community by no choice of their own.

What he is, in relation to the encompassing society, is therefore not a member of a class of that society, because he stays deliberately apart from it. He is following a career pattern based upon jobs available to him within that society's system of production. Like the 'spiralists' of the encompassing society, he is moving from one place to another in search of better opportunities, and like them, his social identity is not defined by relations within a specific local community but by a certain relation to such local communities in general. It is precisely by staying apart from the local society itself that this relation is maintained.

I have tried to show why it seems advantageous for the
immigrant to keep to the values of the encompassed society,
even when these values - as is the case with most factory
workers - do not offer him the satisfaction inherent in
being ranked highly in accordance with them. I have also
tried to show that these values are advantageous mainly
to the successful members of the community and that it is
this category which manifestly upholds them.

The main reason for immigration seems to be 'to make
some money', and different encompassing societies are
compared for the niches they offer to Patidars for
exploitation with this view in mind. These statements
seem to add up to some sort of description of the Patidars
as exploiters of English society. There is a certain
element of truth in this. But the business perspective,
which is not only confined to 'business' but extends to
wage labour as well, is the perspective of the immigrant
encompassed society on their adaptation. This is because
it is seen as taking place in an environmental setting,
a setting which is outside the control of the actors of
the encompassed society and therefore can only be rejected
or accepted. The question of what kind of a deal the
employer and English society in general is making does
not enter into the picture. This would involve the
transformation, on the ideological level, of what is seen
as environment into what is seen as interaction, using
these concepts in the way in which I have treated them
earlier. Thus it is possible for a certain job to be
'good money' for somebody arriving here from abroad and
still be underpaid in terms of the values of the encompassing society.

While, therefore, the workers of the encompassing
society may be alienated from the products of their work,
the Patidars are in addition estranged from the society
of which the production is a part. Whereas the British
workers may negate dominant values in British society,
the working Patidars are not bound to these values even
by the principles of negation. Culturally, they have
nothing more in common with their co-worker than with
their bosses.

Desai, using mainly the economic determinant, included
the people he observed in the Midlands in the working
class. I think this is rather misleading, and it certainly
does not fit the people in my study. Neither the Patidars
nor the British workers seem to include the Patidar workers
in this category. In Marx's terminology they would not be
part of the working class since they do not identify
themselves with them. In Weber's terms, they are part
of the working class in the strictly economic sense in so

far as they work in jobs involving such membership. But,
still in Weber's terms, they are not part of the status
group that term themselves 'workers'. But if the
immigrants, as members of their encompassed society, do
not fit into this category, with which groups, occupying
which structural position, within the global society is
it then convenient to compare them?

Thus, I would like to reject the idea of trying to fit
the whole range of people within the encompassed society
into one of the class categories of the encompassing
society. Objective criteria, i.e. in the main economic
criteria, would divide the encompassed society into
classes, as they do when applied to the encompassing
society. It is probably true that in this way most of
its members would be designated 'working-class'. But it
is more relevant, at least to that group of Patidars from
whom I take my material, to understand precisely why this
class split is not recognized.

The estrangement of the Patidar from his work means
that his work status - his economic status within the
English encompassing society's system of production - is
not part of his personal identity in the same way as
would have been the case had the job itself been within
the encompassed society. Again, a certain similarity to
the spiralists of the encompassing society seems clear.

It is because of this barrier of conversion that some
kind of symbiosis emerges. Because of their different
evaluations both the encompassing and the encompassed
society seem to benefit from the deal.

But it will already be perceived that the profit
resulting from the relationship is different in the two
cases. In the case of the encompassed society, it is
the individual actor who finds himself profiting by the
ecology of the encompassing society. He is, quite simply,
deriving more money from it than from comparable
ecologies. For the encompassing society, on the other
hand, the profit is not so clearly individual. It is as
manpower for the encompassing society in general, albeit
for certain firms within it.

The global society is, of course, a capitalist society,
i.e. it is based on the private property of the means of
production, and this ownership includes the right to the
profit made from production by these means. In so far
as the system benefits from the employment of immigrant
labour, the benefit is primarily that of the people in
whose hands rests the ownership of these means. The
benefit to the encompassing society's own working class
are, however, more dubious. To substantiate this point,
a short outline of what I mean by the British working
class is needed.

Whereas the Patidars form part of an upper class in
the Charottar villages and a middle class in Gujarat as a
whole, as well as in East Africa, and see themselves
fundamentally as businessmen, the British workers have a
very different view of their situation. As a working class
they are probably the world's oldest. Theirs is a society
which has for generations been a class society based on
industrial production. The evaluations at the top of this
society have little relevance to their daily life and it
seems more fitting to speak of a distinct 'working-class
culture' in the UK than perhaps in any other country.
The incentive to save is meaningful in a country where
everybody wants to 'become his own boss' ultimately, as
is at least the popular myth of American society. It is
also meaningful in Patidar society, since people insist
on regarding themselves as businessmen. But the British
working class, traditionally, seems to follow a value
system where such mobility is positively devalued. A
passage from Dennis, Henriques and Slaughter (1969, p.35)
about this aspect of working-class culture in Britain
comes to mind:

> This concrete conception of the marks of class is the
> key to the worker's attitude to 'getting on' in the
> world, or what is called upward social mobility. In
> the sense that we have discussed the class relation-
> ship, i.e. structurally, according to position in the
> economic framework, there is an ever dwindling chance
> of mobility for the worker. The tendency is for
> greater concentration in industry, for the cutting-out
> of competition, and thus for the end of the 'little-
> man-who-made-good' days of private enterprise. In
> the basic industries such as coalmining and iron and
> steel, the possibility of a man becoming 'his own
> boss' is nil; it does persist, with important effects
> on class-consciousness in industries such as building.

They go on to give an example of the individual impact
of these tendencies in the case of a miner's son who
became an engineer and, with a gratuity received after
the war, set up his own firm in the building trade. In
time, however, he could not realize the necessary
capital for remaining competitive, and in 1953, he was
in the mines, having tried some other jobs.
Going on to generalize, the authors say (1969, pp.36-7):

> It appears as if the workers cannot attain the status
> and way of life of the upper classes by assuming a
> similar position in the economic system. But in fact
> does anyone want to achieve it? The answer is a result
> of the concrete rather than abstract nature of the
> class distinction. Indeed, the fact that ordinary

workers talk far, far more about the class distinction than they do about the class struggle or other aspects of social class is significant in itself. Propaganda about inequality and injustice has a naturally strong appeal to working people; in all sorts of ways these are the marks of their station in life. Since they can no longer conceive of 'getting on' in the old Samuel Smiles sense they seize on the most conspicuous outward characteristic of the class difference, and this is spending-power, the possession of wealth.

In his work, a man's concern, over and above the minimum of 'holding the job down', is money. Over the past fifteen years money earned at work has raised the miner a certain amount in the social scale within his own class - his family is no longer marked by the poverty of the inter-war years. But 'winning the pools' is the great vision of ending worries and giving a man the chance to decide his own destiny, to be no longer at the mercy of all that his job represents. Money gained in such ways holds out the possibility of breaking down barriers to improvement for the worker and his family.

Obviously enough, the channels of real transformation, such as the treble chance coupon, will carry only the exceptional and fortunate few, and the rest will in the main produce only shortlived and modest improvements. It is a fact that wage-workers remain wage-workers until they are 65. The ideals of behaviour, the good things of life, in short the cultural ends of the society in which they live, remain for most a vision only, in the glossy magazines, the newspapers, on the cinema and the television screen, and in the lives of a few people whom they will never encounter. These 'cultural goals' to borrow expressions from Merton, are not equally available to all participants in the culture because of the inequality of the 'institutionalized means' placed at their disposal.

This can be understood if we assume that in a highly stratified society, if social ties are to be kept, they must either be between relative equals or they must either explicitly deny or imply rank. In order to prevent conflict between rank and kinship or friendship, upward mobility must be checked.

Thus, I turn again to Dennis et al. Writing of the depression of the 1930s, they state (1969, p.80):

In those days nobody was well off, and it is significant that in the 1950s one often hears the phrase, when miners or their wives are discussing some individual who has 'got on' - 'I don't know why he should think so much about himself - his father was only a collier same as anybody else -...' There will follow a detailed description of where the family lived and of experiences shared with them.

However, what is relevant to my point here is that the value system of the British working class is heavily loaded towards spending rather than saving, something the Patidars and other Gujaratis never tire of commenting upon, contrasting it to their own saving ability. A couple of informants actually told me bluntly that what they fear most is the envy of the British working class, directed at this group of strangers making money out of niches from which they themselves barely extract a day-to-day living. This, of course, is not unlike the anti-Jewish sentiments current in many European countries before the war.

The competition between the highly mobile Patidars and the tradition-bound English working class is present at one level; at another level, however, this competition is encompassed by the difference in admission to resources vital for industrial production between both these categories and the owners of the means of production of British class society.

An example is offered by the public transport sector, which, as has often been said, would hardly be operational in England today were it not for the supply of immigrant labour. These jobs are low-paid. Recruitment to these jobs from the encompassing society itself is therefore not sufficient. For immigrants, however, they seem more attractive, and this is partly because of the possibilities of overtime. This is a possibility often rejected by members of the encompassing society because of the social costs involved. For the immigrants, and this is well substantiated by Desai for the Midlands Gujaratis, the overtime becomes an outright asset. The calling for money-making is bound up with a morality for hard work, and overtime thus acquires a social value as well. With overtime, the income from the job is substantially improved, and it seems not unreasonable to argue that the supply of a labour force thus willing to work overtime in effect slows down the process of raising the basic wages in this industry.

From the point of view of the immigrant, then, the encompassing society is seen to offer him niches for exploitation by him. He is converting work done within the context of one evaluational system into goods valued within another. By leaving, for example, the Patidar encompassed community to work and re-entering it with cash

brought from the other system, he is crossing a barrier
of conversion. The profit stems from the difference in
values: the overtime work which in English society would
be looked upon unfavourably by his mates and by his family
becomes a prestige item within his own social setting.

I have tried here to treat the situation of the
Patidars in relation to the British from the point of view
of the general model suggested by Barth. I have tried to
show how this special relation, described as encompassment,
can be seen to result (at least partly) from the values
(summarized in ethnicity) of the actors, and the
constraints laid upon them by British society, already
there as something to which the immigrants had to adapt.
But I have also tried to show that though the constraints
imposed by the environment may perhaps be objectively
described, and seen as independent valuables, they become
active factors in generating the observed form only
through being perceived by the actors, and thus it is
not ecology 'in itself', but the view of the environment
that the actors have, what they perceive as ecological
constraints as against strategic constraints, that is
active as a factor in the generative model.

In this way, the relative isolation of the encompassed
community from the encompassing society is seen as a
result of a particular ideological interpretation of the
opportunity situation in which the Patidars find themselves.

The implications of this for the analysis of urban
ethnicity in general must be that the opportunity situation, as viewed by the actors from among the 'minority',
'immigrant group', etc., ought to be given a central
position in the analysis.

Into this opportunity situation enter the ecological
conditions (i.e. those that stem from real physical
conditions), and the historical determinants that might
be translated as constraints for the actors which are of
essentially the same kind as those of ecology. At the
same time 'ideology' enters into the analysis as being
the subjective viewpoint from which the actors view
these constraints. The constraints might thus well be
viewed quite differently by actors from different
communities.

The ethnic boundary, as it influences the actors'
choices, may be seen as just this kind of synthesis
between ideology and ecology. It is there, and can be
used for economic purposes; but at the same time it is
itself part of the ideology and in the last instance
depends upon the actor's willingness to accept it. And
it is not possible to say objectively how an 'ethnic

boundary' should be drawn; my suggestion, however, is
that such a boundary might be defined, for analytical
purposes, as the line between those people with whom
interaction is seen as taking place, and those to whom
the actors have an attitude, making them part of the
'environment'.

Where minority communities, whether depressed or not,
find themselves drawing such a line, while the majority
controls the territory and keeps the access to all
significant statuses within the division of labour, I
speak of the situation being one of 'encompassment'.
This excludes cases of real ethnic stratification, where
the division of labour is ethnically based, as it does
also the 'plural society' situation where no single
ethnic group is in full control either of the territory
or of the division of labour, though one group may control
the formal political apparatus.

To show how the ethnic boundary may be drawn in
different ways by different groups, let me compare, very
briefly, the Patidars with the Sikhs, as described by
Thompson (1970), Aurora (1969), John (1969) and Marsh
(1967).

In the case of the Patidars the ethnic boundary is
closely bound up with the 'merchant ideology'. In a
sense the Patidars are seen as different from the English
because they are business-minded. In the case of the
Sikhs, however, there is no such 'merchant ideology'.
Thus being a Sikh does not seem to conflict with accepting
the identity of a labourer, and I would suggest that
this is one reason why Sikhs have been forming 'Indian
Workers' Associations' in many places, while Patidars
have not made much of themselves in trade unions. The
Sikhs, at least in Coventry, have also taken up some of
the customs of the British working man, for many go to
pubs and use them like the English. When Coventry
Gujaratis go to pubs, and that is very seldom indeed,
they generally visit only the saloon bar, keeping away
from the 'common' workers. Much the same is true of
most London Patidars.

I would hold that this kind of behaviour stems from
a different interpretation of the same ecological
conditions. Sikhs see their opportunities in terms of
obtaining the best conditions possible as labourers, and,
alternatively, aspire to a different kind of employment
through education. Patidars see their opportunities
largely in terms of 'business' and the popularity of
accountancy as a career for young Patidars suggests that
this influences their attitude to education too.

Both Sikhs and Patidars keep themselves distant from

the English, and thus there is a clear ethnic boundary in both cases. But whereas the Patidars have drawn theirs in such a way as to keep themselves away from 'working-class' identification, the Sikhs have formed organizations on this very foundation. They have therefore entered into a relation to the encompassing society rather different from that of the Gujaratis.

A similar comparison might be made between the Patidars and the Ismailis. Personal information from Roger Hallam – who has studied London Ismailis – suggests that they view their opportunity situation more in terms of high-status white-collar careers, and though they, like the Patidars, are business-minded they prefer managerial positions in large companies to small-scale business of their own. This means that their attitudes are rather more similar to those of English middle-class people, and though they, too, maintain an ethnic boundary it has not the same implications for individual economic behaviour as has that of the Patidars. Thus to an outsider they seem more 'integrated' into British society.

Through these few examples I have tried to show briefly how encompassed communities within English society may be compared by keeping the actors' view of the opportunity situation in focus. I hope I have shown, however sketchily, the usefulness of this approach.

While there is evidence that the present adaptation of the Patidars to the encompassing society is fruitful to them, I have indicated the danger that their very success might spark off ill-feeling of a similar kind to that to which the European Jews have been subject. I do not think that such an ill-feeling is right or justified, but I do think that the dangers inherent in the present situation might fruitfully be discussed by the Patidars themselves.

A short note on names and castes

In this book I have used fictive names. Names, however, often carry considerable social meaning in India; thus some general points should be made clear.

Most Patidars carry the surname Patel. In this book, I have used that surname without changing it, since it is so common that it is hardly possible to identify any person from the use of that name alone. I have changed other surnames used in the caste to Patel wherever they appear, since these names are much less common. In giving my informants fictive names I have tried to keep to names that I know Patidars use.

All Patels are not Patidars, however. Patidars originally belonged to the Kanbi caste but have set themselves apart from it, a matter discussed more closely in chapter 3. In a few places I refer to people of the Kanbi caste. This refers always to people who are not Patidars and who come from other districts of Gujarat - mainly Saurashtra or the south.

In some cases I have used first names only. Where nothing else is specifically stated, these are Patidars.

The surnames Modi and Shah are used by the Bania caste, i.e. the merchant castes, and I have used them for people belonging to that caste.

Names used for children, like Aku and Baku, are not proper names but pet-names denoting, in this case, the first and second son born.

Desai is both a caste name and a family name, so the people called Desai in the book all belong to that caste. Desais are Brahmins, but they are also landowners and they are not priests. There exists an excellent monograph on the caste by Van der Veen (1972).

Some caste designations appear from time to time in the text. Mostly a brief explanation is given. It will do no harm, however, to mention some of them here. Rajputs are

a martial landowning caste in the northern and western
(Saurashtra) parts of Gujarat state. In Charottar, however,
the home of the Patidars, they have lost their landowner-
ship to the Patidars and have become their tenants
(chapter 3). Lohanas are traders in Saurashtra, the only
trading caste not to be included in the category of
Banias. In England they rank below Patidars. The Banias
proper - the merchant castes - are important as they have
come to constitute the 'model' for Patidar emancipation.
Thus they rank above Patidars, the only caste of
importance in London beside the Desai Brahmins to do so.
Lohars are blacksmiths, and rank well below the Patidars.

A final mention should be made of certain regularities
in the use of names among Patidars. Non-Gujarati readers
may be surprised by the common use of initials - I.P.,
P.J., etc. Such designation is common in the community.
It is mainly used for 'householders', i.e. family heads.
The same is to a considerable extent true of the suffix
'bhai', which means 'brother' but carries no implication
of kinship. 'Bhai' is also used as a term of address,
and would then be used mainly to people who are not too
different from the speaker in terms of rank.

When a first name is used here without this suffix,
the person indicated is unmarried. This is not a strict
rule, but probably rather common practice among Patidars.

The suffix '-bai' means, literally, a woman. As a
rule here it is used only for married women, and this
again corresponds to common usage though not to a rule.

Notes

INTRODUCTION

1 Ideology I take to be a rather more narrow concept
   than culture. Whereas I am using ideology to describe
   evaluations according to which strategies are
   conceived, I take culture to be the sum total of
   knowledge available to the individual.
2 The difference indicated here may be made slightly
   more clear by saying that waste of money is wrong
   rather than stupid. The similarities to 'the Protestant
   ethic' (Weber, 1930, pp.47-92) are evident, but that
   similarity (and the possible differences) cannot be
   discussed here.
3 Playing chess, Baku was talking of the queen as the
   most 'expensive' piece in the game. It was tempting
   to look further for idioms of a mercantile origin in
   Gujarati culture, but I did not feel that my Gujarati
   was adequate for such a study. Basing himself partly
   upon such a study of idioms, Prins (1965, pp.263-75)
   has coined the term 'maritime culture' and relates it
   to Bateson's concept of 'ethos' (1958, p.118). It
   seems likely that a 'merchant ethos' might be found
   in Gujarati culture, and discussions with my friend,
   the Gujarati anthropologist Rohit Barot, seem to
   substantiate this assumption. But again, such a study
   would far exceed the bounds of this book.
4 It is interesting to note that he claimed to have
   chosen this particular car because of its fuel economy.
5 A 'namaskar' is the traditional Hindu greeting, the
   hands lifted in front of the face, with the fingertips
   together and the palms facing each other. It may or
   may not be accompanied by the greeting, 'Namaste' or
   'Namasteji'.

6 This information derives mainly from personal communication with Mark Thompson, then finishing his fieldwork among Sikhs in Coventry. A Sikh worker running a shop on the side, if I have understood him rightly, would be likely to say that the shop was just a side activity - perhaps run by the women. For the Jats in Coventry, the identification with the farming tradition of the Jats was much more important (see also Thompson, 1970).

7 'Function' is used here in its Indian English meaning. It denotes a festive occasion, a celebration, usually attended by a considerable number of people.

CHAPTER 1 THE PROBLEM

1 Community is a word which has been much misused. Thompson (1970, pp.29-30), however, seems to me to put it rather well, and my use of the concept is similar to his:

> Community ... has become a relative term depending for its reference on the standpoint of the observer. To English citizens of Coventry there is an immigrant community, to West Indians there is an Indian community, to Gujaratis there is a Punjabi community, to Jats there is a Ram Gharia community, and so on. 'Community' implies in the eyes of the outsider a corporate group with a degree of consciousness and coactivity - but this impression may be completely erroneous.
>
> However, the popular usage can be given a technical definition. In Coventry there is a comprehensive network of relations that extends throughout the city within which primary, and, to a large extent, secondary relations of Punjabis are restricted. With reference to any individual the network is unbounded, but as a whole it is bounded in that it extends only to include the local Punjabi population of several thousands. Some individuals and subgroups are marginal to this network in that they have a limited number of links leading into it, but through the network of links almost any Punjabi can 'fix' in a social position almost any other. All the members of the network make up the Punjabi community. It corresponds exactly with what is popularly regarded as such.

2 (1970, pp.159-60):

> race relations situations and problems have the following characteristics: they refer to situations

in which two or more groups with distinct identities
and recognizable characteristics are forced by
economic or political circumstance to live together
in a society. Within this they refer to situations
in which there is a high degree of conflict between
the groups and in which ascriptive criteria are used
to mark out the members of each group in order that
one group may pursue one of a number of hostile
policies against the other. Finally within this
group of situations true race relations situations
may be said to exist when the practices of ascriptive allocation of roles and rights referred to are
justified in terms of some kind of deterministic
theory, whether that theory be of a scientific,
religious, cultural, historical, ideological or
sociological kind and whether it is highly
systemized, or exists only on the everyday level of
folk wisdom or in the foreshortened factual or
theoretical models presented by the media.

3   The identification and tolerance needed for
integration can be achieved through two processes:
assimilation and accommodation. The first leads
to identification, the second leads to a tolerance
of differences (Desai, 1963, p.147).

I do not necessarily imply, however, by using the term,
that integration, even in this sense, is the necessary
outcome; this will be clear from the last chapter of
this book. When I use the term, therefore, the stress
is on the maintenance of differences as opposed to
identification with the host society.

CHAPTER 2   THE PATIDARS' BACKGROUND

1   The number of villages in the lower marriage circles
seem somewhat confused. Twenty-one and twenty-seven
were those given by my informants. Pocock's twenty-
six may or may not refer to the same circle.   It is
not improbable, in fact, that some confusion about the
actual number of villages in the lower circles is
shared by the Patidars themselves, resulting in
conflicting information: neither can it be ruled out
that there is actually some 'inclusion and exclusion'
going on, so that the number of villages in each circle
indeed changes from time to time.

CHAPTER 3   THE PATIDARS IN BRITAIN

1   'Objective situation' is of course a misleading use
    of words, but has been used since it seems difficult
    to find a better one. It might be defined as 'the
    sum total of potential energy sources', but this does
    not help us here, since in extending the use of
    ecological terms to inter-ethnic situations we leave
    the field where 'energy' is simply to be reckoned in
    calories. What I mean, then, is just that it seems
    correct to distinguish between the situation as it
    might be seen by someone holding the key to all
    relevant facts, and as seen by members of a certain
    immigrant group who are very far from having such
    complete knowledge. The 'objective situation' thus
    remains hypothetical, but is not therefore necessarily
    unimportant.
2   The material for the section on jobs is taken from a
    number of sources, notably Patterson, 1965; Rose et al.,
    1969; Foot, 1965; Davison, 1966; and Butterworth, ed.,
    1967.

Bibliography

AMIN, R.K. 1 (n.d.; ?1960-7), 'Mogri', Vallabh Vidyanagar: Vallabh Vidyanagar Vidyapith.
AMIN, R.K. 2 (n.d.; ?1960-7), 'Valasan', Vallabh Vidyanagar: Vallabh Vidyanagar Vidyapith.
AURORA, G.S. (1967), 'The New Frontiersman', Bombay: Popular Prakashan.
BAILEY, F.G. (1959), For a sociology of India?, in 'Contributions to Indian Sociology', III.
BAILEY, F.G. (1969), 'Stratagems and Spoils', Oxford: Blackwell.
BANTON, M. (1967), 'Race Relations', London: Tavistock.
BARNES, J.A. (1954), Class and committees in a Norwegian island parish, 'Human Relations', 7, 39-58.
BARTH, F. (1956), Ecologic relationships of ethnic groups in Swat, north Pakistan, 'American Anthropologist', 5, 1079-89.
BARTH, F. (1959), Segmentary opposition and the theory of games: a study of Pathan organization, 'Journal of the Royal Anthropological Institute', 89, pt 1.
BARTH, F. (ed.) (1963), 'The Role of the Entrepreneur in Social Change in Northern Norway', Bergen and Oslo: Norwegian Universities Press.
BARTH, F. (1964), Competition and symbiosis in north east Baluchistan, 'Folk', 6 (1), 15-22.
BARTH, F. (1966), 'Models of Social Organization', London: Royal Anthropological Institute, Occasional paper no.23.
BARTH, F. (1967), Economic spheres in Darfur, in R. Firth (ed.), 'Themes in Economic Anthropology', ASA Monographs no. 6, London: Tavistock.
BARTH, F. (ed.) (1969), 'Ethnic Groups and Boundaries', Oslo: Scandinavian University Books.
BARTH, F. (1971), Minoritetsproblem från socialantropologisk synspunkt, in D. Schwarz (ed.), 'Identitet och Minoritet', Stockholm: Almkvist and Wiksell.

144

BARTH, F. (1972a), Analytical Dimensions in the Comparison of Social Organization, 'American Anthropologist', vol.74, pp.207-19.
BARTH, F. (1972b), Synkron komparasjon, in 'Studier i Historisk Metode', VI: 'Analyse-Syntese-Komparasjon', Oslo: Universitetsforlaget.
BARTH, F. (1973), Descent and marriage reconsidered, in J. Goody (ed.), 'The Character of Kinship', Cambridge University Press.
BASHAM, A.L. (1967), 'The Wonder that was India', Calcutta: Fontana.
BATESON, G. (1958), 'Naven', 2nd ed., Stanford University Press.
BERREMAN, G.D. (1962), 'Behind Many Masks', Society for Applied Anthropology Monographs no.4, Ithaca, N.Y.
BLOM, J.-P. (1969), Ethnic and Cultural Deviation, in F. Barth (ed.) (1969).
BOHANNAN, P. (1963), 'Social Anthropology', New York: Holt, Rinehart & Winston.
BOTTOMORE, T.B. and RUBEL, M. (eds) (1963), 'Karl Marx: Selected Writings in Sociology and Social Philosophy', Harmondsworth: Pelican.
BROX, O. (1972), Komparativ analys av marginella lokalsamhällen, in 'Strukturfascismen och andra essäer', Uppsala: Prisma.
BURNEY, E. (1967), 'Housing on Trial', London: Oxford University Press for the Institute of Race Relations.
BUTTERWORTH, E. (ed.) (1967), 'Immigrants in West Yorkshire: Social Conditions and the Lives of Pakistanis, Indians and West Indians', London: Institute of Race Relations, Special Series.
CENSUS OF INDIA (n.d.), vol.5, pt 6, no.11, Village Survey Monographs: Ambav.
COHEN, A. (1969), 'Custom and Politics in Urban Africa', Berkeley: University of California Press.
DAVISON, R.B. (1966), 'Black British: Immigrants to England', London: Oxford University Press for Institute of Race Relations.
DENNIS, N., HENRIQUES, C.F. and SLAUGHTER, C. (1969), 'Coal is our Life', paperback, London: Tavistock.
DESAI, R.H. (1963), 'Indian Immigrants in Britain', London: Oxford University Press for the Institute of Race Relations.
DUMONT, L. (1957), For a sociology of India, 'Contributions to Indian Sociology', no.1.
DUMONT, L. (1966), 'Homo Hierarchicus', Paris: Gallimard.

DUMONT, L. (1967), Caste: a phenomenon of social structure or an aspect of Indian culture?, in A.V.S. de Reuck and J. Knight (eds), 'Caste and Race: Comparative Apparatus', CIBA Foundation, London: Churchill.

EIDHEIM, H. (1963), Entrepreneurship in Politics, in F. Barth (ed.) (1963).

ELKAN, W. (1960), 'Migrants and Proletarians', London: Oxford University Press.

FOOT, P. (1965), 'Immigration and Race in British Politics', Penguin Special.

FREILICH, M. (ed.), 1970), 'Marginal Natives: Anthropologists at Work', New York: Harper & Row.

FRANKENBERG, R. (1966), 'Communities in Britain', Penguin.

FUCHS, S. (1965), 'Rebellious Prophets', London: Asia.

GOFFMAN, E. (1959), 'The Presentation of Self in Everyday Life', New York: Doubleday Anchor.

HAALAND, G. (1969), Economic determinants in ethnic processes, in F. Barth (ed.) (1969).

HABERMAS, J. (1968), 'Technik und Wissenschaft als Ideologie', Frankfurt am Main: Suhrkamp.

HARRER, H. (1953), 'Syv ar i Tibet', Oslo: Johan Grundt Tanum.

JOHN, D. (1969), 'Indian Workers' Associations in Britain', London: Oxford University Press for Institute of Race Relations.

LAMB, H. (1939), The Indian merchant, in M. Singer (ed.), 'Traditional India: Structure and Change', Philadelphia: American Folklore Society.

LEACH, E.R. (1954), 'Political Systems of Highland Burma', London: LSE Monographs.

LYONS, M. (1971), Indian Migration into Britain, Department of Sociology, University of Aberdeen (duplicated).

McPHERSON, K. and GAITSKELL, J. (1969), 'Immigrants and Employment: Two Case Studies in East London and Croydon', London: Institute of Race Relations, Special Series.

MARSH, P. (1969), 'The Anatomy of a Strike: Unions, Employers, and Punjabi Workers in a Southall Factory', London: Institute of Race Relations, Special Series.

MAYER, A.C. (1957), Factions in Fiji Indian Rural Settlements, 'British Journal of Sociology', vol.8, no.4, pp.317-28.

MAYER, A.C. (1959), A Report on the East Indian Community in Vancouver, working paper, Institute of Social and Economic Research, University of British Columbia, Vancouver.

MAYER, A.C. (1960), 'Caste and Kinship in Central India: a village and its Region', London: Weidenfeld & Nicolson.

MAYER, A.C. (1963), 'The Indians in Fiji', London: Oxford University Press for the Institute of Race Relations.

MAYER, A.C. (1967), Patrons and brokers in overseas Indian communities, in M. Freedman (ed.), 'Social Organization', London, Cass.

MORRIS, S. (1968), 'Indians in Uganda: Caste and Sect in a Plural Society', London: Weidenfeld & Nicolson.

MUNSHI, K.M. (1954), 'Gujarat and its Literature', vol.1, Bombay: Bharatiya Vidya Bhavan.

MURPHY, R.J. and KASDAN, L. (1968), The Structure of Parallel Cousin Marriage, in P. Bohannan and J. Middleton, 'Marriage, Family and Residence', Garden City, N.Y.: Natural History Press.

MYRDAL, G. (1954), 'An American Dilemma': vol.1, 'The Negro in a White Nation', paperback, New York: McGraw-Hill.

MYRDAL, J. (1967), 'Report from a Chinese Village', Penguin.

NAIPAUL, V.S. (1964), 'An Area of Darkness', London: Deutsch.

PANDIT, M.K. (1965), 'Earning One's Livelihood in Mahuva', London: Asia, for the M.S. University of Baroda.

PATTERSON, S. (1965), 'Dark Strangers: a Study of West Indians in London' (abridged ed.), Penguin.

PEHRSON, R.N. (1966), 'The Social Organization of the Marri Baluch', Chicago: Aldine.

POCOCK, D.F. (1954), The hypergamy of the Patidars, in S.M. Kapadia (ed.), 'Ghurye Felicitation Volume', Bombay: Popular Book Depot.

POCOCK, D.F. (1955), The movement of castes, 'Man', 55, 6.

POCOCK, D.F. (1957a), The bases of faction in Gujarat, 'British Journal of Sociology', 8 (4), 295-306.

POCOCK, D.F. (1957b), Inclusion and exclusion: a process in the caste system of Gujarat, 'Southwestern Journal of Anthropology', 13, 19-31.

POCOCK, D.F. (1957c), 'Difference' in East Africa: a study of caste and religion in modern Indian society, 'Southwestern Journal of Anthropology', 13, 289-300.

POCOCK, D.F. (1973), 'Kanbi and Patidar', London: Oxford University Press.

PRICE, C.A. (1963), 'Southern Europeans in Australia', Sydney: Oxford University Press.

PRINS, A.H.J. (1965), 'Sailing from Lamu: a Study of Maritime Culture in Islamic East Africa', Assen: van Gorcum.

RADCLIFFE-BROWN, A.R. (1952), 'Structure and Function in Primitive Society', London: Cohen & West.

REUCK, A.V.S. de and KNIGHT, J. (eds) (1967), 'Caste and Race: Comparative Approaches', CIBA Foundation, London: Churchill.

REX, J. (1970), 'Race Relations in Sociological Theory',
London: Weidenfeld & Nicolson.
REX, J. and MOORE, R. (1967), 'Race, Community and
Conflict: a Study of Sparkbrook', London: Oxford University
Press for the Institute of Race Relations.
RICHARDS, A.W. (1969), 'The Multicultural States of East
Africa', London: Oxford University Press.
ROSE, E.J.B. et al. (1969), 'Colour and Citizenship: a
Report on British Race Relations', London: Oxford
University Press for Institute of Race Relations.
SAHLINS, M.G. (1961), The Segmentary Lineage: an Organiza-
tion for Predatory Expansion, 'American Anthropologist',
vol.63, pp.322-45.
SHAH, A.M. and SHROFF, R.G. (1958), The Vahivanca Barots
of Gujarat: a caste of genealogists and mythographers,
'Journal of American Folklore', 71, 247-76.
SHAH, P.G. (1961), 'Tribal Life in Gujarat', Bombay:
Bharatiya Vidya Bhavan.
SINHA, S. (1966), Caste in India: its essential pattern
of socio-cultural integration, in A.V.S. de Reuck and
J. Knight, (eds) (1967).
SPATE, O.H.K. and LEARMONTH, A.T.A. (1967), 'India and
Pakistan: a General and Regional Geography', 3rd ed.,
London, Methuen.
SRINIVAS, M.N. (1952), 'Religion and Society among the
Coorgs of South India', London: Oxford University Press.
SRINIVAS, M.N. (1962), A Note on Sanskritization and
Westernization, in 'Caste in Modern India', Bombay: Asia.
TAMBS-LYCHE, H. (1975), A Comparison of Gujarati
Communities in London and the Midlands, 'New Community',
vol.4, pp.349-56.
TAYLOR, G.P. (rev. E.R.L. Lewis) (1944), 'The Student's
Gujarati Grammar', 3rd ed., Surat.
THOMPSON, M. (1970), A Study of Generation Differences in
Immigrant Groups with Special Reference to Sikhs, M.Phil.
thesis for the University of London.
VAN DER VEEN, K. (1972), 'I give Thee my Daughter',
Assen: V. Gorcum.
WAGLEY, C. and HARRIS, M. (1958), 'Minorities in the New
World', New York: Columbia University Press.
WEBER, M. (1930), 'The Protestant Ethic and the Spirit
of Capitalism', trans. Talcott Parsons, New York: Charles
Scribner; London: Allen & Unwin.
WEBER, M. (1964), 'The Theory of Social and Economic
Organization', trans. A.M. Henderson and Talcott Parsons,
ed. Talcott Parsons, paperback, New York: Free Press.
WEBER, M. (1967), Class, status and party, in R. Bendix
and S.M. Lipset (eds), 'Class, Status and Power', 2nd ed.,
London: Routledge & Kegan Paul.
YOUNG, M. and WILLMOTT, P. (1962), 'Family and Kinship in
East London', Harmondsworth: Penguin.

Index

Routledge Social Science Series

Routledge & Kegan Paul   London, Henley and Boston

39 Store Street, London WC1E 7DD
Broadway House, Newtown Road,
Henley-on-Thames, Oxon RG9 1EN
9 Park Street, Boston, Mass. 02108

International Library of Sociology

General Editor John Rex

GENERAL SOCIOLOGY

Barnsley, J. H. The Social Reality of Ethics. *464 pp.*
Brown, Robert. Explanation in Social Science. *208 pp.*
● Rules and Laws in Sociology. *192 pp.*
Bruford, W. H. Chekhov and His Russia. *A Sociological Study. 244 pp.*
Burton, F. and **Carlen, P.** Official Discourse. *On Discourse Analysis, Government Publications, Ideology. About 140 pp.*
Cain, Maureen E. Society and the Policeman's Role. *326 pp.*
●**Fletcher, Colin.** Beneath the Surface. *An Account of Three Styles of Sociological Research. 221 pp.*
Gibson, Quentin. The Logic of Social Enquiry. *240 pp.*
Glucksmann, M. Structuralist Analysis in Contemporary Social Thought. *212 pp.*
Gurvitch, Georges. Sociology of Law. *Foreword by Roscoe Pound. 264 pp.*
Hinkle, R. Founding Theory of American Sociology 1883-1915. *About 350 pp.*
Homans, George C. Sentiments and Activities. *336 pp.*
Johnson, Harry M. Sociology: *a Systematic Introduction. Foreword by Robert K. Merton. 710 pp.*
●**Keat, Russell** and **Urry, John.** Social Theory as Science. *278 pp.*
Mannheim, Karl. Essays on Sociology and Social Psychology. *Edited by Paul Kecskemeti. With Editorial Note by Adolph Lowe. 344 pp.*
Martindale, Don. The Nature and Types of Sociological Theory. *292 pp.*
●**Maus, Heinz.** A Short History of Sociology. *234 pp.*
Myrdal, Gunnar. Value in Social Theory: *A Collection of Essays on Methodology. Edited by Paul Streeten. 332 pp.*
Ogburn, William F. and **Nimkoff, Meyer F.** A Handbook of Sociology. *Preface by Karl Mannheim. 656 pp. 46 figures. 35 tables.*
Parsons, Talcott, and **Smelser, Neil J.** Economy and Society: *A Study in the Integration of Economic and Social Theory. 362 pp.*
Podgórecki, Adam. Practical Social Sciences. *About 200 pp.*
Raffel, S. Matters of Fact. *A Sociological Inquiry. 152 pp.*
●**Rex, John.** (Ed.) Approaches to Sociology. *Contributions by Peter Abell,* Sociology and the Demystification of the Modern World. *282 pp.*
●**Rex, John** (Ed.) Approaches to Sociology. *Contributions by Peter Abell, Frank Bechhofer, Basil Bernstein, Ronald Fletcher, David Frisby, Miriam Glucksmann, Peter Lassman, Herminio Martins, John Rex, Roland Robertson, John Westergaard and Jock Young. 302 pp.*
Rigby, A. Alternative Realities. *352 pp.*
Roche, M. Phenomenology, Language and the Social Sciences. *374 pp.*
Sahay, A. Sociological Analysis. *220 pp.*

Strasser, Hermann. The Normative Structure of Sociology. *Conservative and Emancipatory Themes in Social Thought. About 340 pp.*
Strong, P. Ceremonial Order of the Clinic. *About 250 pp.*
Urry, John. Reference Groups and the Theory of Revolution. *244 pp.*
Weinberg, E. Development of Sociology in the Soviet Union. *173 pp.*

FOREIGN CLASSICS OF SOCIOLOGY

● **Gerth, H. H.** and **Mills, C. Wright.** From Max Weber: *Essays in Sociology. 502 pp.*
● **Tönnies, Ferdinand.** Community and Association. *(Gemeinschaft and Gesellschaft.) Translated and Supplemented by Charles P. Loomis. Foreword by Pitirim A. Sorokin. 334 pp.*

SOCIAL STRUCTURE

Andreski, Stanislav. Military Organization and Society. *Foreword by Professor A. R. Radcliffe-Brown. 226 pp. 1 folder.*
Carlton, Eric. Ideology and Social Order. *Foreword by Professor Philip Abrahams. About 320 pp.*
Coontz, Sydney H. Population Theories and the Economic Interpretation. *202 pp.*
Coser, Lewis. The Functions of Social Conflict. *204 pp.*
Dickie-Clark, H. F. Marginal Situation: *A Sociological Study of a Coloured Group. 240 pp. 11 tables.*
Giner, S. and **Archer, M. S.** (Eds.). Contemporary Europe. *Social Structures and Cultural Patterns. 336 pp.*
● **Glaser, Barney** and **Strauss, Anselm L.** Status Passage. *A Formal Theory. 212 pp.*
Glass, D. V. (Ed.) Social Mobility in Britain. *Contributions by J. Berent, T. Bottomore, R. C. Chambers, J. Floud, D. V. Glass, J. R. Hall, H. T. Himmelweit, R. K. Kelsall, F. M. Martin, C. A. Moser, R. Mukherjee, and W. Ziegel. 420 pp.*
Kelsall, R. K. Higher Civil Servants in Britain: *From 1870 to the Present Day. 268 pp. 31 tables.*
● **Lawton, Denis.** Social Class, Language and Education. *192 pp.*
McLeish, John. The Theory of Social Change: *Four Views Considered. 128 pp.*
● **Marsh, David C.** The Changing Social Structure of England and Wales, 1871-1961. *Revised edition. 288 pp.*
Menzies, Ken. Talcott Parsons and the Social Image of Man. *About 208 pp.*
● **Mouzelis, Nicos.** Organization and Bureaucracy. *An Analysis of Modern Theories. 240 pp.*
Ossowski, Stanislaw. Class Structure in the Social Consciousness. *210 pp.*
● **Podgórecki, Adam.** Law and Society. *302 pp.*
Renner, Karl. Institutions of Private Law and Their Social Functions. *Edited, with an Introduction and Notes, by O. Kahn-Freud. Translated by Agnes Schwarzschild. 316 pp.*

Rex, J. and **Tomlinson, S.** Colonial Immigrants in a British City. *A Class Analysis. 368 pp.*

Smooha, S. Israel: Pluralism and Conflict. *472 pp.*

Wesolowski, W. Class, Strata and Power. *Trans. and with Introduction by G. Kolankiewicz. 160 pp.*

Zureik, E. Palestinians in Israel. *A Study in Internal Colonialism. 264 pp.*

SOCIOLOGY AND POLITICS

Acton, T. A. Gypsy Politics and Social Change. *316 pp.*

Burton, F. Politics of Legitimacy. *Struggles in a Belfast Community. 250 pp.*

Etzioni-Halevy, E. Political Manipulation and Administrative Power. *A Comparative Study. About 200 pp.*

⬤**Hechter, Michael.** Internal Colonialism. *The Celtic Fringe in British National Development, 1536–1966. 380 pp.*

Kornhauser, William. The Politics of Mass Society. *272 pp. 20 tables.*

Korpi, W. The Working Class in Welfare Capitalism. *Work, Unions and Politics in Sweden. 472 pp.*

Kroes, R. Soldiers and Students. *A Study of Right- and Left-wing Students. 174 pp.*

Martin, Roderick. Sociology of Power. *About 272 pp.*

Myrdal, Gunnar. The Political Element in the Development of Economic Theory. *Translated from the German by Paul Streeten. 282 pp.*

Wong, S.-L. Sociology and Socialism in Contemporary China. *160 pp.*

Wootton, Graham. Workers, Unions and the State. *188 pp.*

CRIMINOLOGY

Ancel, Marc. Social Defence: *A Modern Approach to Criminal Problems. Foreword by Leon Radzinowicz. 240 pp.*

Athens, L. Violent Criminal Acts and Actors. *About 150 pp.*

Cain, Maureen E. Society and the Policeman's Role. *326 pp.*

Cloward, Richard A. and **Ohlin, Lloyd E.** Delinquency and Opportunity: *A Theory of Delinquent Gangs. 248 pp.*

Downes, David M. The Delinquent Solution. *A Study in Subcultural Theory. 296 pp.*

Friedlander, Kate. The Psycho-Analytical Approach to Juvenile Delinquency: *Theory, Case Studies, Treatment. 320 pp.*

Gleuck, Sheldon and **Eleanor.** Family Environment and Delinquency. *With the statistical assistance of Rose W. Kneznek. 340 pp.*

Lopez-Rey, Manuel. Crime. *An Analytical Appraisal. 288 pp.*

Mannheim, Hermann. Comparative Criminology: *a Text Book. Two volumes. 442 pp. and 380 pp.*

Morris, Terence. The Criminal Area: *A Study in Social Ecology. Foreword by Hermann Mannheim. 232 pp. 25 tables. 4 maps.*

Podgorecki, A. and **Łos, M.** Multidimensional Sociology. *About 380 pp.*

Rock, Paul. Making People Pay. *338 pp.*

● **Taylor, Ian, Walton, Paul,** and **Young, Jock.** The New Criminology. *For a Social Theory of Deviance. 325 pp.*

● **Taylor, Ian, Walton, Paul** and **Young, Jock.** (Eds) Critical Criminology. *268 pp.*

SOCIAL PSYCHOLOGY

Bagley, Christopher. The Social Psychology of the Epileptic Child. *320 pp.*

Brittan, Arthur. Meanings and Situations. *224 pp.*

Carroll, J. Break-Out from the Crystal Palace. *200 pp.*

● **Fleming, C. M.** Adolescence: Its Social Psychology. *With an Introduction to recent findings from the fields of Anthropology, Physiology, Medicine, Psychometrics and Sociometry. 288 pp.*

● The Social Psychology of Education: *An Introduction and Guide to Its Study. 136 pp.*

Linton, Ralph. The Cultural Background of Personality. *132 pp.*

● **Mayo, Elton.** The Social Problems of an Industrial Civilization. *With an Appendix on the Political Problem. 180 pp.*

Ottaway, A. K. C. Learning Through Group Experience. *176 pp.*

Plummer, Ken. Sexual Stigma. *An Interactionist Account. 254 pp.*

● **Rose, Arnold M.** (Ed.) Human Behaviour and Social Processes: *an Interactionist Approach. Contributions by Arnold M. Rose, Ralph H. Turner, Anselm Strauss, Everett C. Hughes, E. Franklin Frazier, Howard S. Becker et al. 696 pp.*

Smelser, Neil J. Theory of Collective Behaviour. *448 pp.*

Stephenson, Geoffrey M. The Development of Conscience. *128 pp.*

Young, Kimball. Handbook of Social Psychology. *658 pp. 16 figures. 10 tables.*

SOCIOLOGY OF THE FAMILY

Bell, Colin R. Middle Class Families: *Social and Geographical Mobility. 224 pp.*

Burton, Lindy. Vulnerable Children. *272 pp.*

Gavron, Hannah. The Captive Wife: *Conflicts of Household Mothers. 190 pp.*

George, Victor and **Wilding, Paul.** Motherless Families. *248 pp.*

Klein, Josephine. Samples from English Cultures.
   1. Three Preliminary Studies and Aspects of Adult Life in England. *447 pp.*
   2. Child-Rearing Practices and Index. *247 pp.*

Klein, Viola. The Feminine Character. *History of an Ideology. 244 pp.*

McWhinnie, Alexina M. Adopted Children. *How They Grow Up. 304 pp.*

● **Morgan, D. H. J.** Social Theory and the Family. *About 320 pp.*

● **Myrdal, Alva** and **Klein, Viola.** Women's Two Roles: *Home and Work. 238 pp. 27 tables.*

Parsons, Talcott and **Bales, Robert F.** Family: Socialization and Inter-action Process. *In collaboration with James Olds, Morris Zelditch and Philip E. Slater. 456 pp. 50 figures and tables.*

SOCIAL SERVICES

Bastide, Roger. The Sociology of Mental Disorder. *Translated from the French by Jean McNeil. 260 pp.*

Carlebach, Julius. Caring For Children in Trouble. *266 pp.*

George, Victor. Foster Care. *Theory and Practice. 234 pp.*
Social Security: *Beveridge and After. 258 pp.*

George, V. and **Wilding, P.** Motherless Families. *248 pp.*

● **Goetschius, George W.** Working with Community Groups. *256 pp.*

Goetschius, George W. and **Tash, Joan.** Working with Unattached Youth. *416 pp.*

Heywood, Jean S. Children in Care. *The Development of the Service for the Deprived Child. Third revised edition. 284 pp.*

King, Roy D., Ranes, Norma V. and **Tizard, Jack.** Patterns of Residential Care. *356 pp.*

Leigh, John. Young People and Leisure. *256 pp.*

● **Mays, John.** (Ed.) Penelope Hall's Social Services of England and Wales. *About 324 pp.*

Morris, Mary. Voluntary Work and the Welfare State. *300 pp.*

Nokes, P. L. The Professional Task in Welfare Practice. *152 pp.*

Timms, Noel. Psychiatric Social Work in Great Britain (1939-1962). *280 pp.*

● Social Casework: *Principles and Practice. 256 pp.*

SOCIOLOGY OF EDUCATION

Banks, Olive. Parity and Prestige in English Secondary Education: a Study in Educational Sociology. *272 pp.*

● **Blyth, W. A. L.** English Primary Education. *A Sociological Description.* 2. Background. *168 pp.*

Collier, K. G. The Social Purposes of Education: *Personal and Social Values in Education. 268 pp.*

Evans, K. M. Sociometry and Education. *158 pp.*

● **Ford, Julienne.** Social Class and the Comprehensive School. *192 pp.*

Foster, P. J. Education and Social Change in Ghana. *336 pp. 3 maps.*

Fraser, W. R. Education and Society in Modern France. *150 pp.*

Grace, Gerald R. Role Conflict and the Teacher. *150 pp.*

Hans, Nicholas. New Trends in Education in the Eighteenth Century. *278 pp. 19 tables.*

● Comparative Education: *A Study of Educational Factors and Tra-ditions. 360 pp.*

● **Hargreaves, David.** Interpersonal Relations and Education. *432 pp.*

● Social Relations in a Secondary School. *240 pp.*

School Organization and Pupil Involvement. *A Study of Secondary Schools.*

● **Mannheim, Karl** and **Stewart, W.A.C.** An Introduction to the Sociology of Education. *206 pp.*

● **Musgrove, F.** Youth and the Social Order. *176 pp.*

● **Ottaway, A. K. C.** Education and Society: An Introduction to the Sociology of Education. *With an Introduction by W. O. Lester Smith. 212 pp.*

Peers, Robert. Adult Education: *A Comparative Study. Revised edition. 398 pp.*

Stratta, Erica. The Education of Borstal Boys. *A Study of their Educational Experiences prior to, and during, Borstal Training. 256 pp.*

● **Taylor, P. H., Reid, W. A.** and **Holley, B. J.** The English Sixth Form. *A Case Study in Curriculum Research. 198 pp.*

SOCIOLOGY OF CULTURE

Eppel, E. M. and **M.** Adolescents and Morality: *A Study of some Moral Values and Dilemmas of Working Adolescents in the Context of a changing Climate of Opinion. Foreword by W. J. H. Sprott. 268 pp. 39 tables.*

● **Fromm, Erich.** The Fear of Freedom. *286 pp.*

●   The Sane Society. *400 pp.*

Johnson, L. The Cultural Critics. *From Matthew Arnold to Raymond Williams. 233 pp.*

Mannheim, Karl. Essays on the Sociology of Culture. *Edited by Ernst Mannheim in co-operation with Paul Kecskemeti. Editorial Note by Adolph Lowe. 280 pp.*

Zijderfeld, A. C. On Clichés. *The Supersedure of Meaning by Function in Modernity. About 132 pp.*

SOCIOLOGY OF RELIGION

Argyle, Michael and **Beit-Hallahmi, Benjamin.** The Social Psychology of Religion. *About 256 pp.*

Glasner, Peter E. The Sociology of Secularisation. *A Critique of a Concept. About 180 pp.*

Hall, J. R. The Ways Out. *Utopian Communal Groups in an Age of Babylon. 280 pp.*

Ranson, S., Hinings, B. and **Bryman, A.** Clergy, Ministers and Priests. *216 pp.*

Stark, Werner. The Sociology of Religion. *A Study of Christendom.*
Volume II. *Sectarian Religion. 368 pp.*
Volume III. *The Universal Church. 464 pp.*
Volume IV. *Types of Religious Man. 352 pp.*
Volume V. *Types of Religious Culture. 464 pp.*

Turner, B. S. Weber and Islam. *216 pp.*

Watt, W. Montgomery. Islam and the Integration of Society. *320 pp.*

SOCIOLOGY OF ART AND LITERATURE

Jarvie, Ian C. Towards a Sociology of the Cinema. *A Comparative Essay on the Structure and Functioning of a Major Entertainment Industry. 405 pp.*

Rust, Frances S. Dance in Society. *An Analysis of the Relationships between the Social Dance and Society in England from the Middle Ages to the Present Day. 256 pp. 8 pp. of plates.*

Schücking, L. L. The Sociology of Literary Taste. *112 pp.*

Wolff, Janet. Hermeneutic Philosophy and the Sociology of Art. *150 pp.*

SOCIOLOGY OF KNOWLEDGE

Diesing, P. Patterns of Discovery in the Social Sciences. *262 pp.*

● **Douglas, J. D.** (Ed.) Understanding Everyday Life. *370 pp.*

Glasner, B. Essential Interactionism. *About 220 pp.*

● **Hamilton, P.** Knowledge and Social Structure. *174 pp.*

Jarvie, I. C. Concepts and Society. *232 pp.*

Mannheim, Karl. Essays on the Sociology of Knowledge. *Edited by Paul Kecskemeti. Editorial Note by Adolph Lowe. 353 pp.*

Remmling, Gunter W. The Sociology of Karl Mannheim. *With a Bibliographical Guide to the Sociology of Knowledge, Ideological Analysis, and Social Planning. 255 pp.*

Remmling, Gunter W. (Ed.) Towards the Sociology of Knowledge. *Origin and Development of a Sociological Thought Style. 463 pp.*

URBAN SOCIOLOGY

Aldridge, M. The British New Towns. *A Programme Without a Policy. About 250 pp.*

Ashworth, William. The Genesis of Modern British Town Planning: *A Study in Economic and Social History of the Nineteenth and Twentieth Centuries. 288 pp.*

Brittan, A. The Privatised World. *196 pp.*

Cullingworth, J. B. Housing Needs and Planning Policy: *A Restatement of the Problems of Housing Need and 'Overspill' in England and Wales. 232 pp. 44 tables. 8 maps.*

Dickinson, Robert E. City and Region: *A Geographical Interpretation. 608 pp. 125 figures.*
The West European City: *A Geographical Interpretation. 600 pp. 129 maps. 29 plates.*

Humphreys, Alexander J. New Dubliners: *Urbanization and the Irish Family. Foreword by George C. Homans. 304 pp.*

Jackson, Brian. Working Class Community: *Some General Notions raised by a Series of Studies in Northern England. 192 pp.*

● **Mann, P. H.** An Approach to Urban Sociology. *240 pp.*

Mellor, J. R. Urban Sociology in an Urbanized Society. *326 pp.*

Morris, R. N. and **Mogey, J.** The Sociology of Housing. *Studies at Berinsfield. 232 pp. 4 pp. plates.*

Rosser, C. and **Harris, C.** The Family and Social Change. *A Study of Family and Kinship in a South Wales Town. 352 pp. 8 maps.*

● **Stacey, Margaret, Batsone, Eric, Bell, Colin** and **Thurcott, Anne.** Power, Persistence and Change. *A Second Study of Banbury. 196 pp.*

RURAL SOCIOLOGY

Mayer, Adrian C. Peasants in the Pacific. *A Study of Fiji Indian Rural Society. 248 pp. 20 plates.*

Williams, W. M. The Sociology of an English Village: *Gosforth. 272 pp. 12 figures. 13 tables.*

SOCIOLOGY OF INDUSTRY AND DISTRIBUTION

Dunkerley, David. The Foreman. *Aspects of Task and Structure. 192 pp.*

Eldridge, J. E. T. Industrial Disputes. *Essays in the Sociology of Industrial Relations. 288 pp.*

Hollowell, Peter G. The Lorry Driver. *272 pp.*

● **Oxaal, I., Barnett, T.** and **Booth, D.** (Eds) Beyond the Sociology of Development. *Economy and Society in Latin America and Africa. 295 pp.*

Smelser, Neil J. Social Change in the Industrial Revolution: *An Application of Theory to the Lancashire Cotton Industry, 1770–1840. 468 pp. 12 figures. 14 tables.*

Watson, T. J. The Personnel Managers. *A Study in the Sociology of Work and Employment. 262 pp.*

ANTHROPOLOGY

Brandel-Syrier, Mia. Reeftown Elite. *A Study of Social Mobility in a Modern African Community on the Reef. 376 pp.*

Dickie-Clark, H. F. The Marginal Situation. *A Sociological Study of a Coloured Group. 236 pp.*

Dube, S. C. Indian Village. *Foreword by Morris Edward Opler. 276 pp. 4 plates.*

India's Changing Villages: *Human Factors in Community Development. 260 pp. 8 plates. 1 map.*

Firth, Raymond. Malay Fishermen. *Their Peasant Economy. 420 pp. 17 pp. plates.*

Gulliver, P. H. Social Control in an African Society: a Study of the Arusha, Agricultural Masai of Northern Tanganyika. *320 pp. 8 plates. 10 figures.*

Family Herds. *288 pp.*

Jarvie, Ian C. The Revolution in Anthropology. *268 pp.*

Little, Kenneth L. Mende of Sierra Leone. *308 pp. and folder.*

Negroes in Britain. *With a New Introduction and Contemporary Study by Leonard Bloom. 320 pp.*

Madan, G. R. Western Sociologists on Indian Society. *Marx, Spencer, Weber, Durkheim, Pareto. 384 pp.*

Mayer, A. C. Peasants in the Pacific. *A Study of Fiji Indian Rural Society. 248 pp.*

Meer, Fatima. Race and Suicide in South Africa. *325 pp.*

Smith, Raymond T. The Negro Family in British Guiana: *Family Structure and Social Status in the Villages. With a Foreword by Meyer Fortes. 314 pp. 8 plates. 1 figure. 4 maps.*

SOCIOLOGY AND PHILOSOPHY

Barnsley, John H. The Social Reality of Ethics. *A Comparative Analysis of Moral Codes. 448 pp.*

Diesing, Paul. Patterns of Discovery in the Social Sciences. *362 pp.*

● **Douglas, Jack D.** (Ed.) Understanding Everyday Life. *Toward the Reconstruction of Sociological Knowledge. Contributions by Alan F. Blum, Aaron W. Cicourel, Norman K. Denzin, Jack D. Douglas, John Heeren, Peter McHugh, Peter K. Manning, Melvin Power, Matthew Speier, Roy Turner, D. Lawrence Wieder, Thomas P. Wilson and Don H. Zimmerman. 370 pp.*

Gorman, Robert A. The Dual Vision. *Alfred Schutz and the Myth of Phenomenological Social Science. About 300 pp.*

Jarvie, Ian C. Concepts and Society. *216 pp.*

Kilminster, R. Praxis and Method. *A Sociological Dialogue with Lukács, Gramsci and the early Frankfurt School. About 304 pp.*

● **Pelz, Werner.** The Scope of Understanding in Sociology. *Towards a More Radical Reorientation in the Social Humanistic Sciences. 283 pp.*

Roche, Maurice. Phenomenology, Language and the Social Sciences. *371 pp.*

Sahay, Arun. Sociological Analysis. *212 pp.*

Slater, P. Origin and Significance of the Frankfurt School. *A Marxist Perspective. About 192 pp.*

Spurling, L. Phenomenology and the Social World. *The Philosophy of Merleau-Ponty and its Relation to the Social Sciences. 222 pp.*

Wilson, H. T. The American Ideology. *Science, Technology and Organization as Modes of Rationality. 368 pp.*

International Library of Anthropology

General Editor   Adam Kuper

Ahmed, A. S. Millenium and Charisma Among Pathans. *A Critical Essay in Social Anthropology. 192 pp.*
  Pukhtun Economy and Society. *About 360 pp.*

Brown, Paula. The Chimbu. *A Study of Change in the New Guinea Highlands. 151 pp.*

Foner, N. Jamaica Farewell. *200 pp.*

Gudeman, Stephen. Relationships, Residence and the Individual. *A Rural Panamanian Community. 288 pp. 11 plates, 5 figures, 2 maps, 10 tables.*

The Demise of a Rural Economy. *From Subsistence to Capitalism in a Latin American Village. 160 pp.*

Hamnett, Ian. Chieftainship and Legitimacy. *An Anthropological Study of Executive Law in Lesotho. 163 pp.*

Hanson, F. Allan. Meaning in Culture. *127 pp.*

Humphreys, S. C. Anthropology and the Greeks. *288 pp.*

Karp, I. Fields of Change Among the Iteso of Kenya. *140 pp.*

Lloyd, P. C. Power and Independence. *Urban Africans' Perception of Social Inequality. 264 pp.*

Parry, J. P. Caste and Kinship in Kangra. *352 pp. Illustrated.*

Pettigrew, Joyce. Robber Noblemen. *A Study of the Political System of the Sikh Jats. 284 pp.*

Street, Brian V. The Savage in Literature. *Representations of 'Primitive' Society in English Fiction, 1858–1920. 207 pp.*

Van Den Berghe, Pierre L. Power and Privilege at an African University. *278 pp.*

International Library of Social Policy

General Editor Kathleen Jones

Bayley, M. Mental Handicap and Community Care. *426 pp.*

Bottoms, A. E. and **McClean, J. D.** Defendants in the Criminal Process. *284 pp.*

Butler, J. R. Family Doctors and Public Policy. *208 pp.*

Davies, Martin. Prisoners of Society. *Attitudes and Aftercare. 204 pp.*

Gittus, Elizabeth. Flats, Families and the Under-Fives. *285 pp.*

Holman, Robert. Trading in Children. *A Study of Private Fostering. 355 pp.*

Jeffs, A. Young People and the Youth Service. *About 180 pp.*

Jones, Howard, and **Cornes, Paul.** Open Prisons. *288 pp.*

Jones, Kathleen. History of the Mental Health Service. *428 pp.*

Jones, Kathleen, with **Brown, John, Cunningham, W. J., Roberts, Julian** and **Williams, Peter.** Opening the Door. *A Study of New Policies for the Mentally Handicapped. 278 pp.*

Karn, Valerie. Retiring to the Seaside. *About 280 pp. 2 maps. Numerous tables.*

King, R. D. and **Elliot, K. W.** Albany: Birth of a Prison—End of an Era. *394 pp.*

Thomas, J. E. The English Prison Officer since 1850: *A Study in Conflict.* *258 pp.*

Walton, R. G. Women in Social Work. *303 pp.*

● **Woodward, J.** To Do the Sick No Harm. *A Study of the British Voluntary Hospital System to 1875. 234 pp.*

International Library of Welfare and Philosophy

General Editors   Noel Timms and David Watson

● **McDermott, F. E.** (Ed.) Self-Determination in Social Work. *A Collection of Essays on Self-determination and Related Concepts by Philosophers and Social Work Theorists. Contributors: F. B. Biestek, S. Bernstein, A. Keith-Lucas, D. Sayer, H. H. Perelman, C. Whittington, R. F. Stalley, F. E. McDermott, I. Berlin, H. J. McCloskey, H. L. A. Hart, J. Wilson, A. I. Melden, S. I. Benn. 254 pp.*

● **Plant, Raymond.** Community and Ideology. *104 pp.*

Ragg, Nicholas M. People Not Cases. *A Philosophical Approach to Social Work. About 250 pp.*

● **Timms, Noel** and **Watson, David.** (Eds) Talking About Welfare. *Readings in Philosophy and Social Policy. Contributors: T. H. Marshall, R. B. Brandt, G. H. von Wright, K. Nielsen, M. Cranston, R. M. Titmuss, R. S. Downie, E. Telfer, D. Donnison, J. Benson, P. Leonard, A. Keith-Lucas, D. Walsh, I. T. Ramsey. 320 pp.*

● (Eds). Philosophy in Social Work. *250 pp.*

● **Weale, A.** Equality and Social Policy. *164 pp.*

Primary Socialization, Language and Education

General Editor   Basil Bernstein

Adlam, Diana S., *with the assistance of Geoffrey Turner and Lesley Lineker.* Code in Context. *About 272 pp.*

Bernstein, Basil. Class, Codes and Control. *3 volumes.*

● 1. *Theoretical Studies Towards a Sociology of Language. 254 pp.*

2. *Applied Studies Towards a Sociology of Language. 377 pp.*

● 3. *Towards a Theory of Educational Transmission. 167 pp.*

Brandis, W. and **Bernstein, B.** Selection and Control. *176 pp.*

Brandis, Walter and **Henderson, Dorothy.** Social Class, Language and Communication. *288 pp.*

Cook-Gumperz, Jenny. Social Control and Socialization. *A Study of Class Differences in the Language of Maternal Control. 290 pp.*

● **Gahagan, D. M** and **G. A.** Talk Reform. *Exploration in Language for Infant School Children. 160 pp.*

Hawkins, P. R. Social Class, the Nominal Group and Verbal Strategies. *About 220 pp.*

Robinson, W. P. and **Rackstraw, Susan D. A.** A Question of Answers. *2 volumes. 192 pp. and 180 pp.*

Turner, Geoffrey J. and **Mohan, Bernard A.** A Linguistic Description and Computer Programme for Children's Speech. *208 pp.*

Reports of the Institute of Community Studies

Baker, J. The Neighbourhood Advice Centre. A Community Project in Camden. *320 pp.*

● **Cartwright, Ann.** Patients and their Doctors. *A Study of General Practice. 304 pp.*

Dench, Geoff. Maltese in London. *A Case-study in the Erosion of Ethnic Consciousness. 302 pp.*

Jackson, Brian and **Marsden, Dennis.** Education and the Working Class: *Some General Themes raised by a Study of 88 Working-class Children in a Northern Industrial City. 268 pp. 2 folders.*

Marris, Peter. The Experience of Higher Education. *232 pp. 27 tables.*

● Loss and Change. *192 pp.*

Marris, Peter and **Rein, Martin.** Dilemmas of Social Reform. *Poverty and Community Action in the United States. 256 pp.*

Marris, Peter and **Somerset, Anthony.** African Businessmen. *A Study of Entrepreneurship and Development in Keyna. 256 pp.*

Mills, Richard. Young Outsiders: *a Study in Alternative Communities. 216 pp.*

Runciman, W. G. Relative Deprivation and Social Justice. *A Study of Attitudes to Social Inequality in Twentieth-Century England. 352 pp.*

Willmott, Peter. Adolescent Boys in East London. *230 pp.*

Willmott, Peter and **Young, Michael.** Family and Class in a London Suburb. *202 pp. 47 tables.*

Young, Michael and **McGeeney, Patrick.** Learning Begins at Home. *A Study of a Junior School and its Parents. 128 pp.*

Young, Michael and **Willmott, Peter.** Family and Kinship in East London. *Foreword by Richard M. Titmuss. 252 pp. 39 tables.*

The Symmetrical Family. *410 pp.*